GOSSIP *and the* GOSPEL

GOSSIP *and the* GOSPEL

Their throats are open graves; their tongues practice deceit.
The poison of vipers is on their lips. – Romans 3:13

WINEPRESS WP PUBLISHING

Published by WinePress Publishing, PO Box 428, Enumclaw, WA 98022.

ISBN 1-57921-757-5
Library of Congress Catalog Card Number: 2004094257

Presented Out of Love

This book is given to:

____

in hopes they will repent of the sin of gossip, slur, slander, or bitter roots.

> For I am afraid that when I come I may not find you as I want you to be, and you may not find me as you want me to be. I fear that there may be quarreling, jealousy, outbursts of anger, factions, slander, gossip, arrogance and disorder. (2 Corinthians 12:20)

Dedicated to those who love God enough not to think evil of each other.

In your hearts do not think evil of each other.
(Zechariah 7:10b)

A Prayer

Lord, we ask You to crucify our flesh, to place a guard over our lips that we may never sin against You or man who was made in Your image. Oh Lord, do not drag us away with the wicked, with those who do evil, who speak cordially with their neighbors but harbor malice in their hearts. Open our eyes to any malice hiding in the dark shadows of our hearts that we might confess it as sin and find healing in Your wonderful light.

Yes, Lord, do not drag us away in judgment because of the sin of our tongues.

> Do not drag me away with the wicked, with those who do evil, who speak cordially with their neighbors but harbor malice in their hearts. (Psalm 28:3)

Amen

Contents

Make it your ambition
to lead a quiet life,
to mind your own business . . .
—1 Thessalonians 4:11

Introduction

Gossip is sin. The church has forgotten that gossip is a vile sin before God. So vile a sin, that the apostle Paul commanded us not to even have lunch with a gossiper or slanderer.[1] The Greek word for slander is taken from diabolos, which means devil. The message of this book is that gossip, slander, and bitter roots are deadly sins that we cannot tolerate. This book primarily focuses on how, within the church, gossip undermines the true gospel message. We will see how gossip and evil suspicions can keep us from a church God calls us to fellowship with. We will discuss how the sinful nature of even the redeemed can still fall prey to the evil power of gossip. It is a look at gossip and the gospel.

While we all know that gossip is sin, gossip can also demonstrate that a church preaches the gospel. For the Holy Spirit to guide us to a church where we should worship, we will have to tune out the gossip in order to hear the voice of

God's Truth. Jesus came to bring division[2] and when it comes to the true gospel, gossip will naturally divide true lovers of God from false Christians—the sheep from the goats.

This book really presents a basic question. Which side are you on? There is no middle ground when it comes to gossip and the gospel. We are either slandered, or are party to those who slander. For he who is not for Jesus, scatters.[3] Which side would you have been on? With the apostles or the Jews? With those who receive slander, or the slanderers?

> The people of the city were divided; some sided with the Jews, others with the apostles. (Acts 14:4)

Any church worth its salt in Jesus will have far more enemies than members. The Holy Spirit will direct and empower the God's Word to strike at the very heart of a person's sin—the thing self is most attached to. God does this so that He might personally kill self and replace it with the image of His Son. Since the vast majority of individuals, including those in the church, will not surrender these things to God, they leave blaming the messenger. Seldom will people, when lovingly confronted with sin, admit that they have hard hearts. Instead, they attack a godly church, especially the leadership. For example, an individual came to visit the church I pastor. It was clear to all, except to the man himself, that pride was his overwhelming sin. Like so many, he used praying about it as a cover to justify his unwillingness to see and surrender the sin. He said things like, "I can't confess sins I cannot see." Which on the surface of things is a fair statement. We never ask an individual to repent of something they do not see as sin. This does not, however, excuse them from guilt, but simply shows that they are too hard hearted to accept what the Holy Spirit speaks to them. In the end, the individual did not tell others "They are right, I am loaded with pride, but am too hard hearted to see or admit it." Rather, he resorted to gossip, slander, and ultimately to a bitter root that led him to go around telling others that unless they personally agree with me, the pastor, I tell them they will go to hell. His full implication was that I am a cult leader who must be fully obeyed in everything if you want to be considered a Christian. Such absurd lies and outright slander will happen to any church where God shows Himself to be holy, where the Holy Spirit reveals sin that must go. This feels uncomfortable, to say the least, for most individuals—and so they spread gossip that there is something strange about that particular group or church. That strangeness, in reality, is holiness which such people are fully alienated from. To discover the joy of the narrow road, any seeker of God will have to move way past this huge crowd of gossipers in order to find the true gospel.

One of the good fruits of a true church of Jesus is the plotters of persecution—hounds that seek to sniff out anything to discredit the message of the cross. In short, follow the gossip if you want to find a godly church. Any true church of Jesus will be slandered. While every church slandered may not be of God, people will gossip about every true church following Jesus. To find Jesus, you will have to join a church that others gossip about—there is no way around it. If you declare that no one gossips about your church then you need to move closer to Jesus. Ask the Holy

Spirit to deal with sin in your church, striking at the very self in each person, and everything mentioned in this book will happen to you.

There will always be those who consider it their Pharisaic duty to dig up any dirt they can find—or make any good deed seem dirty. Indeed, no matter how good an act or deed, such men and women will persecute it and seek to discredit it.

> Then he said to the man, "Stretch out your hand." So he stretched it out and it was completely restored, just as sound as the other. But the Pharisees went out and plotted how they might kill Jesus. (Matthew 12:13–14)

Think of it, Jesus healed a man—what a good deed! But the only reaction of the Pharisees was to plot against Jesus. If you find a church in your area that experiences this, ask God for wisdom. They may be following Jesus.

CHAPTER I

World of Evil

"Okay, now pick up the phone and give them a call," I gently instructed my sons. Often as we sat around the dinner table we discussed many things in the Lord. One of my sons wrote a song entitled, *Here at the Table*[1] about these and many other God-directed experiences at dinner time.

Sometimes the children relayed stories about something "bad" someone else did. At that point, I would ask if they talked to the person about it and they would answer, "No." It didn't take my sons, and guests, long to learn that if they complain about someone else they need to talk directly to that person. This of course caused my sons—from a very young age—to watch their words and their hearts, and to make sure their words flowed from a heart filled with the love of the Holy Spirit.[2] In our home, we understand the sin of talking evil about others comes as natural as the fires of hell, so we strive to carefully weigh our words.

> The tongue also is a fire, a world of evil among the parts of the body. It corrupts the whole person, sets the whole course of his life on fire, and is itself set on fire by hell. (James 3:6)

The tongue contains the fire of hell. Hell overflows with gossiping, slandering beings who constantly slur each other. We corrupt ourselves by talking about others. How we use the tongue demonstrates to the discerning whether a man lays a course bound for heaven or hell. For this reason, Scripture says a man lives a worthless religion who does not use his tongue in love and keep a "tight reign" on what he says. Many, as James 1:26 states, totally deceive themselves about the holiness of their Christianity. Indeed, many an expert or discernment ministry provides nothing but a cover for hellish speech. Then there are those that everyone identifies as the gossipers in their church. From the folly of our own tongues, to organizations that thrive on gossip, we must, by the grace of God, confront this sin head on.

Defining the Sin

Let's define some terms related to gossip.

- A comment becomes a *slur* when we cast the slightest shadow upon the goodness of another without asking if the Holy Spirit is in that particular statement. For example, someone compliments another and someone else makes an unflattering statement to remind listeners that the person isn't all *that* good.
- Our words turn into *gossip* when we talk about someone concerning personal sins against us but have not

gone to them first.[3] Or for entertainment we like to gossip or talk about other's lives.

- *Slander* means you use information to prove *your* point or to support *your* position in a matter. Even if correct, it's still slander when we refuse to allow the cross to crucify our flesh.
- A *false witness* sees something but alters the facts just enough to fit their own needs.
- And a *bitter root* occurs when the above four have grown to the point that bitterness pervades all that is said and done.

Gossip is still sin even if something is proven factual or true, because the gossiper's heart promotes evil rather than love. Truth does not simply make gossip godly. Such an attitude demonstrates a heart that follows Satan, because even he quotes Scripture—God's truth.

This book will not attempt to deal with the sin of gossip in the world, but within the church. The world will always back-bite and slander one another. Christians, however, act like fools when we seek to prove our doctrine by attacking the character of our opponent. In short, those that claim to be Christians should know better. We fall into complete sin and folly when we seek to avoid the sin in our own lives by pointing out a sin in another's.

Careless Words

Any discussion about others is sin if we haven't surrendered self to the Lord to be crucified. It is sin to not hate our own lives[4] and deny ourselves. Those who do not hate their own lives seek to puff themselves up by slurring, ever so slightly, the character of others. Without death to self and hating our own life, our offer to help others only ends in causing a great deal of harm. God will call us to account for every careless word we speak

> But I tell you that men will have to give account on the day of judgment for every careless word they have spoken. (Matthew 12:36)

Whenever we spread slander, whether we think it true or not, we endanger others. We do not know for sure what evil will happen because we have spread something. Therefore, even as early as the Old Testament, God said that if you have something against your neighbor you should be frank about it with them. In New Testament terms that means to "walk in the light" by the power of the Holy Spirit.[5]

Every day we should set the goal not to do anything that endangers our neighbor. I say goal, because if we do not determine this, by nature we will bring harm to our neighbor. We must remember our sinful natures. Our throats are open graves; we practice deceit with our tongues, and have the poison of vipers resting on our lips. We, by nature, when we speak, already have a graveyard of dead things we have said resting in our mouths. For example, telling tales just a tad bit more exciting than reality to draw attention to us as storytellers. And of course, do not forget the sinful excitement that comes from declaring the faults of others. Lying about the things we say, practicing to say something deceitful so others cannot realize the full truth, and injecting our poisonous talk into others—that is who we are without the cross crucifying us.

> "Their throats are open graves; their tongues practice deceit." "The poison of vipers is on their lips." "Their mouths are full of cursing and bitterness." (Romans 3:13–14)

We must also guard our hearts so that we never hate those we talk about, and never carry or act out a grudge.

If our neighbor does not see the sin we bring to them we must not seek revenge or even bear a grudge. If we actively go after someone we will sin greatly against the Lord, no matter how right we think our cause. We must prayerfully lay the matter before God to deal with in His timing and truth.

> Do not go about spreading slander among your people. Do not do anything that endangers your neighbor's life. I am the Lord. Do not hate your brother in your heart. Rebuke your neighbor frankly so you will not share in his guilt. Do not seek revenge or bear a grudge against one of your people, but love your neighbor as yourself. I am the Lord. (Leviticus 19:16–18)

Betraying a Confidence

Often many who leave churches spread personal things about others to prove the church wrong or because some sin was revealed in their own lives and they feel angry. What a grievous sin in the sight of God. When we argue our case it should stand on the merits of truth, not upon personally attacking others.

> If you argue your case with a neighbor, do not betray another man's confidence. (Proverbs 25:9)

We should avoid taking advantage of what we know personally about someone when proving our point. Not only does this betray a confidence, the opposite of love that always protects, but we could easily be mistaken. Our own sins and prejudices could blind us to the truth. In the end, the living God will rebuke those who ignore or rebel against this instruction. You can be sure they will not go unpunished.

Mind Your Own Business

All Christians should make it their ambition to lead a quiet life and to mind their own business, as the following passage emphasizes.

> Make it your ambition to lead a quiet life, to mind your own business and to work with your hands, just as we told you. (1 Thessalonians 4:11)

It takes a mighty strong ambition to mind one's own business today in the church. Only if the Holy Spirit makes something our business should we talk about it or move forward in the matter. Jesus knew when things were not His business or His concern. These same words should often come from the lips of His disciples, because we too must stay out of everything that God does not make our business. I often hear the Holy Spirit repeat this scripture in my heart when individuals ask me for decisions. Many times I will tell someone,

"I don't know," and ask them not to concern me with the issue but to go work it out with God.

> Jesus replied, "Man, who appointed me a judge or an arbiter between you?" (Luke 12:14)

It's a Small World

The world closes in on us in ever increasing ways. New technologies carry information at greater and greater speed, which means that, as Christians, we need self-discipline more than ever so as not to abuse such things. With the Internet it only takes mere seconds to spread something around, to vent our bitterness that defiles hundreds. How much harm has already been done to the church of Jesus because we spout things off without giving it a second thought, let alone to pray about it before the cross? Wait for the Lord before writing or saying anything and you will spare yourself from sinning.[6]

Not one time did Peter, Paul, James, or John go around exposing the sins of other groups or individuals in the name of preaching the gospel. In fact, when an issue arose they didn't gossip about it on their way to Jerusalem, but resolved to preach the cross and only the cross.[7] We have become a world of snoops being told the lie that it benefits others when we trample on people's privacy. But we often do not know all the facts, and what at first appears wrong, may very well be of God. Take a car wreck for example. Two people can witness it but come to some very different descriptions as to how it happened. How much more could this be true with spiritual matters of the cross?

> The first to present his case seems right, till another comes forward and questions him. (Proverbs 18:17)

Sometimes when the Holy Spirit leads me to point out the sin of others, they will whine that I am gossiping or slandering. They cannot tell the nature of my comments because they do not know the power of the cross. The difference between speaking wrongly against others and when the Holy Spirit leads someone to speak is like the difference between a man who walks into a store and pulls a deadly gun out and when a policeman pulls his weapon.

Jesus said that towards the end of the last days the love in the church will grow cold because wickedness will increase sharply. The Internet, magazines, television, and telephones inflame the sin of gossip. Since gossip has become the norm on such an exaggerated scale, we now think of it as part of regular conversation. Individuals can gather together quickly and efficiently like never before, thus creating an unhealthy environment for uplifting conversation in the Lord to survive. At each moment multitudes of Christians stand ready to jump in with, "I think . . ." But as Proverbs 18:2 declares, only a fool delights in airing his own opinion.

Today within the church, we seem to only call something gossip when we do not want to hear it or it affects us personally. In short, justice is not our concern. We must deal with gossip without any hint of favoritism[8]—rebuking it no matter how we respect the person speaking or how badly we want to hear it.

We should thoroughly test such matters of God's will by the cross and hating our own lives. We should always speak in the Light, never saying to someone, "Don't tell others I told you." To ask someone to do this is sin and causes another person to sin also. When individuals ask me to keep it just between us, I tell them not to say another word, because in the Lord, they must be willing to come into the Light and take full responsibility for what they plan to tell me. I know when to keep a confidence, but cannot ever guarantee a permanent confidence.[9] If it benefits the love of Christ, it will be told; if not now, certainly at the end of time.[10]

As a Pastor, those who come to me never feel assured that what they say will not be brought into the Light. As Christians, not only should they know better, but realize the love of Christ demands that holiness rule the day. In fact, if they honestly repent of their sin, why would they feel afraid? Now, I know when, in the Holy Spirit, to keep a secret, but harboring unrepentant sinners does not please a holy God.

In fact, we please God when we rise out of bed each day and silence those who whisper gossip in the ears of others. God is not pleased when, in the name of grace, we endure those who slander their neighbor in secret. In short, do you want to please God? Then silence those who gossip and do not endure those who slander.

> Whoever slanders his neighbor in secret, him will I put to silence; whoever has haughty eyes and a proud heart, him will I not endure. (Psalm 101:5)

Jesus said those who remain in the darkness with their comments and actions fear exposure of their sins and you can be sure they are up to no good.

> Everyone who does evil hates the light, and will not come into the light for fear that his deeds will be exposed. (John 3:20)

To not reveal the name of someone who told you gossip makes you an accessory in the crime before God. When you go to someone about something you have heard you must begin by telling them who you heard it from—otherwise it would be sin to deal with the issue any further. Satan loves darkness and the kind of blackness that spreads gossip by saying, "They made me promise not to tell my source,"—such promises are vows unto Satan. It is an act of cruelty to keep secret the name of a gossiper. It places the people gossiped about at a terrible disadvantage. Not only do stories become perverted, but the person has no way to set the record straight at the source of the slander. Even if the person repeating the gossip tells the source it is not true, questions are left unanswered, and hearts need cleansing by confession and repentance of sin.

All repentance of sin, from the Old Testament through the New was done out in the open. Even the sacrifices for sin, under the Old Covenant, were burnt in the temple and everyone knew that a person paid the price for their sins. A person who sinned did not stay at home and ask for forgiveness in a darkened prayer closet. This is why the New Covenant commands us to surpass the Law and walk in the Light.

As children most of us have played the game called Gossip. Take a room full of thirty people and whisper in the first person's ear a piece of gossip. Then have them whisper to the person next to them, doing this one by one until all thirty people have heard the whispered message. Have the last person declare what he or she heard. What happens? The final message seldom sounds anything like the original.

God will severely judge people who agree not to reveal a gossip source but it will go well with those who convict such individuals. Indeed, rich blessings will be upon those who keep everything in the Light.

> But it will go well with those who convict the guilty, and rich blessing will come upon them. (Proverbs 24:25)

Think of how much gossip could be stopped if everyone, in every church, ministry, and home required a name attached to whatever they repeat. And what repentance and love could flow if we always went to a person before gossiping about him or her. How pleased God would be if this rule of love became the norm among Christians. In Jesus there are no anonymous sources—that is the way of this dark world.

> There is nothing concealed that will not be disclosed, or hidden that will not be made known. (Luke 12:2)

CHAPTER 2

An Art Form

They make their tongues as sharp as a serpent's; the poison of vipers is on their lips. Selah (Psalm 140:3)

Gossip is an art form to many. They practice their deceit, refining every word to make it fit their needs.[1] They make their tongues sharp and venomous as a serpent, manufacturing within their mouths ever increasing deadly poison. Poison drips from their lips and kills whoever accepts their words.

I remember an individual who put down her cross and in bitterness declared, "The truth and love are in this church, but there is something wrong that I can't put my finger on."

When I heard this and responded the next day, pointing out the obvious—that Jesus said truth and love were exactly the two things[2] that demonstrate someone comes from God, she changed her words. With her own words this woman revealed that the church she held bitterness against really came from God. However, instead of repenting, she sharpened her tongue and made a deadlier poison. She then declared that we do not love at all. The kindness and love shown to her by the church became twisted into something vile and evil.[3] With renewed zeal, she poisoned and paralyzed others.

The "something" she complained about was the offense of the cross[4] that produces the good fruit of love and joy in a church. Most people never think such love is possible, and many more do not want it, so others naturally assume the worst. False witnesses use this ignorance against others just as Satan uses his knowledge of God against the ignorance of man.

Be Reconciled

For this reason, whenever we listen to someone's complaint we need to stop them at the start and ask, "Did you go privately to this person and speak one on one and give them a chance to repent?" If the answer is no, rebuke the tale bearer sharply and move on.

> If your brother sins against you, go and show him his fault, just between the two of you. If he listens to you, you have won your brother over. But if he will not listen, take one or two others along, so that "every matter may be established by the testimony of two or three witnesses." If he refuses to listen to them, tell it to the church; and if he refuses to listen even to the church, treat him as you would a pagan or a tax collector. (Matthew 18:15–17)

"Just between the two of you," Jesus emphatically said. If you feel that someone in the church has wronged you then you must go to them privately before ever speaking to anyone else about the sin. It doesn't matter if you think it will do any good or not, you must go to that person. Jesus gave no loophole in this matter. When we fail to do this and talk bad of another, we place ourselves squarely in the footsteps of Judas, who used his personal knowledge of Jesus to do harm. How many, like Judas, do not think their schemes will cause any real damage, only to discover later their conversations, gossips, and slurs brought about the troubles of hell for the ones they gossip about? Many are worse off than Judas. At least Judas did not foresee the harm he would cause, while others gossip with the deliberate intention to hurt or damage someone else.

The church resembles a family; very personal and intimate in their understanding of one another. When a relationship is broken it's tempting to use this closeness against those we once loved. In fact, when someone sins against us, we face a great risk that personal wounds will cloud our perception and not allow the love of the Holy Spirit to heal the situation. Love "always" protects.[5] Let us be sure that we make every effort, not the bare minimum, to keep the peace of the Holy Spirit in a church.

> Let us therefore make every effort to do what leads to peace and to mutual edification. (Romans 14:19)

Again, always ask, "Have you gone to this person privately?" If the answer is not a clear "Yes," then shut the conversation down and tell that person to go and do that first. In fact, check back in a couple of days to see if he has done so. Warn that person one more time to go reconcile with his brother. If he refuses, then contact the person he planned to talk about and let him know about the sin. The church must learn to draw attention to those who gossip so that all can take warning.

> So if I come, I will call attention to what he is doing, gossiping maliciously about us. Not satisfied with that, he refuses to welcome the brothers. He also stops those who want to do so and puts them out of the church. (3 John 1:10)

Turn Their Backs

As we approach the end times, just before the antichrist arrives, Jesus said the love of most will grow cold.[6] In this coldness they will deny the faith and hate those they once loved.

> At that time many will turn away from the faith and will betray and hate each other, (Matthew 24:10)

Jesus had many who became disciples, but later turned back and no longer followed Him.[7] This will be true of any church that preaches the narrow gate and road by the power of the Holy Spirit. Those who leave often spread rumors, stories, and tales not because such things are true, but to justify their own unfaithfulness. In fact, it is the first thing they do. They run to their old friends and explain how wicked others acted and claim that nothing was their fault.

They use gossip to whitewash their sins. Because of pride they must explain to others why they stopped following Jesus. Seldom does anyone leave Jesus in honesty stating that they just don't want to be a Christian any longer. I have known several, but not many.

True Christians need to prepare themselves for a whole swarm of gossiping, slandering, and betraying false Christians to fill the church. For in recognizing them now, you will spare yourself following their ways and learn to stand on guard. Do not let your love of man cause you to compromise the demands of Christ, risking rejection by God.

A Godly Church

Follow the trail of those grumbling against a church, and it may just lead to a godly group of people. I can make no promise that such a trail will lead to a godly church, but I can promise that a godly church will be persecuted and gossiped about. Slanders, slurs, a twisting of facts and doctrines and the love that is shown, will be par for the course. The church of the last days will be known by the noticeable increase of the spirit of Judas. Do not let this discourage or dissuade you from a godly church. In fact, let it be one of the good fruits you look for and the rich joy given by the Holy Spirit will be yours.

Jesus, though filled with pure love, was referred to as Beelzebub. People considered Him demonic, a cult leader, and a man with sinister motives who used manipulative powers to win crowds over. This same slander will be said about those who hate their lives enough to fall in love with Jesus. It was true of Paul and it will be true of all godly leaders.[8] This promise, Jesus states, should cause us to leap for joy. Indeed, do not be afraid of slanderers, for God will one day reveal their secret motives and deceived hearts before the whole universe. He will make right every wrong slander, gossip, and the slightest slur. Soon God will make your righteousness shine like the noonday sun.[9] Remember, God judges the wicked first and even with our many faults and sins we will never be put to shame if we remain true to the faith. So fear not when men slander you, rather rejoice and join with those who suffer persecution because they love Jesus. It is a glorious thing to face slander when you pick up your cross and follow Jesus on the narrow road. Since Jesus faced slander, the only way a church cannot be slandered is if they are above Jesus Christ Himself—a spiritual absurdity.

> It is enough for the student to be like his teacher, and the servant like his master. If the head of the house has been called Beelzebub, how much more the members of his household! So do not be afraid of them. There is nothing concealed that will not be disclosed, or hidden that will not be made known. What I tell you in the dark, speak in the daylight; what is whispered in your ear, proclaim from the roofs. (Matthew 10:25–27)

Expect Persecution

Before we consider the sin of slander, let us think again that those who obey Jesus by the power of the Holy Spirit will face the same trials He experienced. For persecution and slander to start, you don't even actually have to live a godly life—you receive it when you really just "want" to imitate Jesus.

> In fact, everyone who *wants* to live a godly life in Christ Jesus will be persecuted, while evil men and impostors will go from bad to worse, deceiving and being deceived. (2 Timothy 3:12–13, emphasis added)

If you surrender to Jesus in all things, expect to be slandered and talked about. As 2 Timothy 3:12–13 tells us, we "will be persecuted," talked about, slandered, and maligned, while others who claim to be Christians remain deceived about their condition and go from "bad to worse." While all this persecution occurs, "evil men," "impostors" in Christ, will be "deceived" about what constitutes true Christianity and therefore set out to deceive others. The deception occurs because such people think they possess the truth while in reality they slander it and those who worship God in truth and in Spirit. So darkened, they honestly believe they do God a favor. This book shows how to guard yourself from being taken in by such people. For God uses evil men to sift His church, to keep it clean from those who refuse to honestly hear His voice by way of the crucified life. Those who don't truly want God, will believe the gossip and avoid the church. This is a blessing in disguise for they would only weaken the church spiritually and waste valuable time while others vainly try to encourage them to live a godly life.

Most churches deserve what people say about them because they practice foolishness or rebel against the commands of God. To possibly claim innocence before God and man when someone talks about you, their accusations must be false. Only slander and gossip that arises out of your obedience to Scripture, as the Holy Spirit leads, can be considered persecution before God. After all, every type of religion experiences persecution and has its own defectors. Every group persecutes the other; Democrat against Republican, Pro-life against Pro-abortion, gun control against the NRA, and so on. True biblical persecution occurs when men hate the righteousness of God and seek to slur the character of those who live godly lives. Rather than let this keep you from such godly leaders and churches, learn to become filled with the joy of the Holy Spirit so you too can "leap for joy."

> Blessed are you when men hate you, when they exclude you and insult you and reject your name as evil, because of the Son of Man. Rejoice in that day and leap for joy, because great is your reward in heaven. For that is how their fathers treated the prophets. (Luke 6:22–23)

Chapter 3

Slurs

Persecution means nothing in and of itself. Look at the following scripture and see that only when Paul preached and lived obedience did the Jews want to kill him.

> First to those in Damascus, then to those in Jerusalem and in all Judea, and to the Gentiles also, I preached that they should repent and turn to God and prove their repentance by their deeds. That is why the Jews seized me in the temple courts and tried to kill me. (Acts 26:20–21)

Preach and live obedience by the Holy Spirit and people will also try to "seize" you. Indeed, if you proclaim that individuals must "prove their repentance by their deeds" you will soon find yourself labeled a legalist. If you demand that others surrender all to the Holy Spirit and actually do something the Spirit calls them to do, you will be slandered with the label of a cult leader or a brainwashed individual. Preach what most churches preach today, live what is lived and your persecution becomes nothing more than one man's opinion against another—merely Sadducee against Pharisee. Gossip about a self-willed church does not indicate godly persecution. Now with that understanding, let us press on to examine closely the sins of slander, gossip, and slurs.

Defining a Slur

We will first take a look at the seriousness of the lesser offense so that we might see the complete wickedness of the greater. To cast the slightest slur against someone keeps you from living on God's holy hill. Recall that a slur casts a shadow on someone's character. It's speaking about someone without asking God if you should. A raised eyebrow at a comment or simple added fact about a person can tarnish someone's character. A slur is a small thing to us, but enough to keep us barred from God's holy hill.

We must make certain before we speak that we declare the truth by the authority and power of the Holy Spirit. We must never judge, for only a fool delights in airing his own opinion.[1] Indeed, unless we despise "a vile man" we will find ourselves taken in by their slander and lose our place in the Book of Life. We must despise those who gossip, especially in the name of the gospel, pleading with them to repent.

> Lord, who may dwell in your sanctuary? Who may live on your holy hill? He whose walk is blameless and who does

> what is righteous, who speaks the truth from his heart and has no slander on his tongue, who does his neighbor no wrong and casts no slur on his fellowman, who despises a vile man but honors those who fear the Lord, who keeps his oath even when it hurts, (Psalm 15:1–4)

It is never enough to just rebuke someone who gossips, we must also "honor" those who fear the Lord. God will not show us the truth in a situation if we harbor the teller of tales in darkness. He never honors disobedience towards love and we must willfully take a stand with those who tell the truth. Often when we confront gossip, those who do not want to deal with the issue falsely accuse us of guilt simply because we defend ourselves. That would be like saying the police are corrupt because they seek to stop crime. The church no longer serves justice and justice alone. Those who love justice will engage in battles not directly waged against them, since selfless love lights the fire of holy zeal.

> Follow justice and justice alone, so that you may live and possess the land the Lord your God is giving you. (Deuteronomy 16:20)

Every little word counts and we must guard ourselves to make sure we bring no wrong against our neighbor. That is why verse four of Psalm 15 said only those who keep their word, even when it "hurts," may live with God on His holy hill.

When we say that we are going to do something people should know we mean what we say. Our yes is yes, and our no is no. In fact, Christians are a people under oath all of the time. In the world, when you go to court, they require that you take an oath to tell the truth, implying that normal conversation is not as true without a pledge. Not so with disciples of Jesus; we speak as if every word comes under an oath. Therefore, James told us "above all things" not to take an oath, or swear (James 5:12). Those who have one standard of conversation for daily life and another for special circumstances will "be condemned." At all times, in all situations, under all circumstances what we say is what we mean and our yes is yes, and no is no.

Many give their word to love, to be a brother or sister in the Lord, only to hate and betray later. They need not question further to know if their salvation remains intact—it is not. They have broken the pledge of all pledges, the sin John said we cannot pray for.[2]

Powerful Words

God made the universe with His word, and created us in His image, so our words carry power. We have the power to bring individuals closer to God and the power to harm them with the smallest comment.

> The tongue has the power of life and death, and those who love it will eat its fruit. (Proverbs 18:21)

To merely cast the slightest "slur" on someone else can keep us from living with God. When we cannot tell the truth about a person or situation, it shows how much of the self-life still exists in us. But to intentionally or accidentally cast even the smallest slur on someone's character calls for the deepest repentance on our part. This doesn't mean we turn a blind eye to the wickedness of others, for recall verse four commands us to despise "a vile man." It does mean if we speak of his vileness, we had better be dead to self and led of the Holy Spirit! Whenever you open your mouth to "help" someone, your soul is at stake as well as theirs. Be mighty careful you are full of the Holy Spirit and in the Light.

Yet how easily we slur and curse others. We mouth off our quick, self-righteous judgments about how "strange," "stubborn," or "sinister" another person seems. We, in our own wisdom and power, voice our opinions about others and their ministry, offering the smallest of criticism. We lift ourselves up so high and often say, "Oh, I like their ministry, but don't agree with everything." We never consider that something might be wrong with our own heart that keeps us from agreeing and being obedient to Scripture. Can you imagine someone saying of Paul, "Well, I like him, but don't agree with everything he does"?

Guard Our Mouths

If we speak of another's sin to benefit ourselves in some way, we become equal to demons. Beware of the slightest turning or slurring of the facts when you speak about someone else or a church. Be on guard against using the pretense of protecting others when it's your own selfish interests you really serve. Make sure it is of the utmost importance that a person knows some particular information. Ask yourself, is this really required? Do they need to know this or would Scripture alone suffice?

Speaking negatively, or for that matter positively, about another person requires the utmost fear and trembling, death to self, wisdom from the Holy Spirit, and God's timing. Such discernment does not come easily or cheaply. So often we feel it our duty to speak of every sin we think we see in someone. How little we know of the love of Christ that leaves many things unsaid until God's timing and grace works His cleansing. Hear from the Holy Spirit to judge nothing before the appointed time of God's will. Even if it is wrong many times it takes years for God to work out a resolution or for the proper time to speak against it.[3]

> Therefore judge nothing before the appointed time; wait till the Lord comes. He will bring to light what is hidden in darkness and will expose the motives of men's hearts. At that time each will receive his praise from God. (1 Corinthians 4:5)

Wrong Conclusions

Often we are wrong in our conclusions about what is sin because our minds have not been transformed, and we use our own biblical knowledge to condemn the innocent. Here's a New Testament example. Joseph, who planned to wed Mary the mother of Jesus, made a false accusation about his fiancé. In fact, he prepared himself to act on his assumption. No doubt he prayed about it, sought the Scriptures, and felt no sense of wrong about divorcing, or "putting away," Mary. Indeed, Joseph had the facts to prove he was correct—Mary was indeed pregnant. God even let Joseph "consider this" fact and conclude that she sinned. This example demonstrates one reason why Jesus said never to judge by "mere appearances."[4]

> This is how the birth of Jesus Christ came about: His mother Mary was pledged to be married to Joseph, but before they came together, she was found to be with child through the Holy Spirit. Because Joseph her husband was a righteous man and did not want to expose her to public disgrace, he had in mind to divorce her quietly. But after he had considered this, an angel of the Lord appeared to him in a dream and said, "Joseph son of David, do not be afraid to take Mary home as your wife, because what is conceived in her is from the Holy Spirit." (Matthew 1:18–20)

Ask yourself, "How many things does God allow me to think I am correct about, when I'm really dead wrong?" To the degree you can honestly answer that question, reveals how clearly you really see others. It shows how you slur others or are taken in by false witnesses.

If you have found yourself slurring someone or a church, search your heart now before God. Do not under your own power examine yourself because I can tell you right now, you will find yourself innocent.

> All a man's ways seem innocent to him, but motives are weighed by the Lord. (Proverbs 16:2)

Just the Facts?

So you think you have the facts about a church, ministry, or person. You researched it well. In fact, you belonged to a particular group. You have made your mind up on the matter because you know the truth and their sin is plain before you. But has God told you it is sin? By the way, even if your flesh should by chance agree with the judgment of God, you are still dead wrong.[5] Those who understand the message of the cross know what I mean. Those who do not, need desperately to find out from God what it means.[6]

Beware of "facts," for they can be simply your own judgments and will always be sinful ones. Just as Joseph used his brain power to conclude the matter about Mary, and by all outward appearances was correct, so you should never conclude anything by your own wisdom. Joseph was a man of humble faith, should we not then walk with great humility?

Most use their own wisdom to find a "comfortable" church and will avoid a church that people slur. Often when looking for a church, people will ask, "What have you heard about that church?" Or, they will search the Internet and see if anyone has a lurid tale to tell. This is especially true when someone who does not agree hears that a friend wants to join a church he or she does not like. We should not listen to the voice of men—after all Satan has a whole army of grumblers to fill our ears. Just think, if you were to ask around about the first church, what kind of reactions would you get?[7]

Never mind the fact that crucifixion never feels comfortable. Those who look for a comfortable church will never find the church God wants for them. For example, if you researched Paul's ministry, listening to gossip with this attitude, you never would have joined him. In fact, the more information you gathered about Paul's ministry, the more confused you would have become about him. For as Paul himself declared, people considered him an "impostor," though he was "genuine" in the Lord. Researching Paul's ministry, because of all the conflicting testimony about him, would have proven futile.

> . . . through glory and dishonor, bad report and good report; genuine, yet regarded as impostors;
> (2 Corinthians 6:8)

Remember, if you want to find the right church, follow the gossip back to a church, and after prayer, go visit that group yourself. First ignore your wisdom and the gossip, and then seek God's wisdom to come to a true conclusion. For in the flesh, we would have all concluded that Paul's ministry was false and he was a troublesome person.[8] Again, any church truly of God will be slandered and talked about. One of Satan's tactics when the truth is preached is to out-shout it by roaring, "It is a cult," "It is evil," or "Strange stories come from that church." Therefore every Christian must move beyond gossip and slander to hear the truth from God.

Seek Righteousness

God stopped Joseph from sinning. Joseph, however, was righteous enough that God could get through to him. His righteousness and pure heart enabled him to hear God speak the truth. Contrast this with another man who asked about the truth. His name was Pilate and he wanted to know the truth about Jesus. It is a sad story. Truth stared Pilate in the face but he could not accept it. In self-pity and despair all Pilate could do was ask, "What is truth?" Though Pilate could find no charge against Jesus, truth could not open up his heart to the love that stood before him. The same is true for the church; many times individuals cannot see the love before them because a sin in their life blinds them.

Many consider fellowshipping at the church I pastor. The truth stares them in the face and they admit they see nothing wrong, but they go out to the rebellious crowds, debate the topic once again, and like Pilate wash their hands of the issue.

> "What is truth?" Pilate asked. With this he went out again to the Jews and said, "I find no basis for a charge against him." (John 18:38)

Although Pilate's wife had a dream about the truth, Pilate did not respond and handed Jesus over to be crucified. He listened to the false witnesses against Jesus and lost his soul. Could God be trying to get through to you, but because you love yourself, you refuse to respond? Do you love the noisy self-righteous crowd of sinning church-goers more than the truth that stands humbly before you?

Again Joseph, a righteous man who could hear God's voice, possessed wisdom no one else in Mary's town could understand.

Just think of the gossip that hit the town where Joseph and Mary lived. *What "kind" of girl did he marry? Joseph clearly compromises the Law. Joseph and Mary are not as holy and pure as everyone thought.* No doubt such thoughts resided in many a heart and were spoken by the lips of gossipers. Once again, we don't often know the whole story of a situation and it is easy enough for others to make something godly look sinister.

In the same way, certain things may appear as "fact," but only those who keep their eyes off of man and on God will know the truth. Many things have been said about our church and ministry and only those who go back into the prayer closet and let God purify their hearts will know the truth. This safeguard helps to dissuade those who give only token obedience to God from joining, and so weakening the church.

Finally even if Joseph had been correct about this issue, notice his attitude. He did not want to "expose her (Mary) to public disgrace." No wonder God spoke to Joseph; he was a man of godly love. How many swiftly run out to complain of their woes, or the failures and questions about another church or person, all in the name of love and concern for others? Indeed, they relish the public disgrace of those they profess to love. What darkness resides in a heart that considers it a duty to warn others at every turn. Like the Devil, such a person can't wait to go public with his thoughts and slight slurs. How unlike the righteous men and women of old. Let us answer the question, who may ascend the hill of the Lord? May we say, by the authority of the Holy Spirit, "We can ascend the hill of the Lord."

> . . . and has no slander on his tongue, who does his neighbor no wrong and casts no slur on his fellowman, (Psalm 15:3)

CHAPTER 4

Poisoned Minds

You cannot reason with a poisoned mind. No matter what you do, no matter how righteous your actions, poisoned people will always view you as wicked. Such minds reflect Satan's for he views everything God does as wicked. Satan really believes the Lord is wicked and seeks to spread the "truth" about God. In the same way, many people believe and view certain groups as wicked. Like Satan, such lies become reality and truth to them. Some are so convinced that their lies are true that they could pass a lie detector test. For, you see, the more you repeat a lie, the harder your heart becomes until you can't discern the truth anymore. For this reason the Psalmist said that God loves a man who speaks the truth "from his heart" by way of a "blameless life."[1]

The next passage shows us how the poisoning of the mind works. In verse 18 Paul demonstrated by his life his

Christ-like humility. Paul did not preach himself, nor was he devious, power hungry, or after money. He was selfless in his love to preach Jesus. In verse 19 some individuals poisoned the minds of those listening to Paul's message. As you read the passage, ask yourself what aspect of sin allowed these men to inject their poison into the crowd? What caused them not to be protected from the serpent's poison? Ask yourself this because you need to see what areas of your flesh are vulnerable to those who inject the poison of slurs, slander, and gossip. For such people will put forth much effort just as the Jews "came from" other cities to win the "crowd over." They will travel, write, contact, and persist in seeking you out in order to slander.

> Even with these words, they had difficulty keeping the crowd from sacrificing to them. Then some Jews came from Antioch and Iconium and won the crowd over. They stoned Paul and dragged him outside the city, thinking he was dead. (Acts 14:18–19)

Vulnerable to Gossip

What sin in these individuals allowed the Jews from Antioch to inject their poison? Do you see the answer? They simply didn't like the humility and loss of self that the cross brings in a man's life. They wanted to offer sacrifices to Paul because this would help them keep their proper self-esteem, life, family, money, pride, fun, doctrine, and religion. Paul demonstrated humility and death to self in his speech and life, but the crowd didn't want to hear that message, for with great "difficulty" Paul kept them from sin.

They wanted to be worshipped, gods of their own life, and rejected anyone who preached the humility of Jesus. Think of it—they rejected Paul because he was humble—such is the vileness of religious man. Do not think you are beyond such twists of persecution. Each of us, without the cross in our life, will come to some very wrong conclusions about the gossip we hear concerning a preacher or a church.

What sins make you easy prey for those who come over to spread slurs and inject poison concerning the gospel truth? Or do you inject yourself with poison so that you don't have to fellowship with those who walk the narrow road? Does something in your spirit tell you that someone is wrong when they may really be very much of God? Or when you left a certain group, did you feel a sigh of relief because you left the cross behind and now slander because of your own unfaithfulness? Let us all be careful not to run from the cross that demands all, otherwise the poison of sinful men shall infect us with their hatred. And we too may turn away from the person God sends to bless us.[2]

Afraid to Join

Again, the crowd did not want to hear Paul's message. The same thing occurs in the church today. In fact, much more so, for now the tree is dry. The church today preaches about the cross, mercy, forgiveness of sins, humility, revival, and denying self, but empties the cross of its power.[3] Today men preach the cross with human fanfare and wisdom. People base their obedience on man's zeal, words, storytelling, preaching, and motivational skills. Indeed, we market revival with all the skill of advertising executives. It is the false revival that God promised would take place. If a church is honestly filled with the holiness of God, then others will feel afraid to join it. Are individuals afraid to join your church because of what the Holy Spirit works in the congregation? If not, why?

> No one else dared join them, even though they were highly regarded by the people. (Acts 5:13)

Those who oppose the message of the cross play to and use this fear to poison the minds of others. Many belong to "The First Church of the Poisoned Mind," and gossip in such a way as to appear concerned for the welfare of others, but such perverse love only ends in separation and suspicion.

> A perverse man stirs up dissension, and a gossip separates close friends. (Proverbs 16:28)

Many a biblical expert or spiritual friend revels in the art of gossip, which only creates an atmosphere of suspicion and quarrelling. They play to the evil suspicions that all of us hold in our hearts, keeping the poison of gossip alive. The slander just goes by nobler sounding names like, "love," "concern," "welfare," "biblical context," or "hermeneutics." We must remember that our flesh, as an enemy of God, often drips honey rather than spits fire. Those who listen to these enemies eagerly swallow their sugar coated poison.[4] Like today, many in the church seek to poison the minds of others against a specific group or church because they are hostile to the true message of Jesus. How many times when the discussion ends, the only fruit remaining is everyone all stirred up? Whether a whisper in the ear, a conference on finding error, or a Bible study, often the bad fruit of stirring people up emotionally is the only real thing accomplished. Does it really take all these ministries to see through the most basic of errors other ministries have? If so, then the church is indeed at an all time low. We really don't need fancy videos, presentations, and book after book about the errors of others. What today's church needs is powerful obedience by the grace of God that naturally reveals sins and errors. In short, if you think someone is in error, then show them by your life and your obedience to God that you have something better. God did not tell us to write books about the errors of a specific church, form a discussion (gossip) group, or have a ministry that devotes its time to accumulating the errors and rumors attached to other ministries. God told us to live a good life. The Lord does not use gossip to spread the truth; He uses obedient children to silence foolish men.

> For it is God's will that by doing good you should silence the ignorant talk of foolish men. (1 Peter 2:15)

> But the Jews who refused to believe stirred up the Gentiles and poisoned their minds against the brothers. (Acts 14:2)

If we could only hear as God hears, we would in an instant tell these individuals to shut up and the fire of gossip and strife would soon die out. Again, those not actively seeking to stop the problem become part of the sin. After all, as Jesus said, he who does not gather, scatters. If the church dealt with gossiper's poison then the Holy Spirit could work true love and peace in our hearts and churches.

> Without wood a fire goes out; without gossip a quarrel dies down. (Proverbs 26:20)

Taking Advantage

Gossip is not a minor sin, and it can cost a person their name in the Book of Life. Sinful individuals make up the church and it takes God time to work His righteousness in us. Consider Abraham or Moses if you need proof in this matter. Working His righteousness in our lives is difficult and, at times, agonizingly slow. God, however, in His love disciplines His sons and daughters, often raising the club and wounding us deeply. Many make sport of those who God hurts and disciplines. They use the weakness of these people to poison the mind of others. In short, they love to gossip with arrows dipped in poison, using what hardship God allows as a weapon. In fact, I know many who, like Satan, eagerly wait for a time when someone becomes weak enough that they can make him or her stumble. Mind you, they don't word it that way. The slanderers speak of rescuing the person, of helping him or her to see the truth and only feel concerned for the struggling person's welfare. The real goal of the gossip is to cause the weak person to leave the church and if they cannot, to make them as weak as possible. Their purpose is not to build anyone up in the crucified life, or joyful obedience to Jesus, but to use the person to do harm to the church and people they betray and hate. The fruit of such actions prove gossipers persecute those God disciplines. One of the more sinister fruits of gossip is to kick someone when they are down.

> For they persecute those you wound and talk about the pain of those you hurt. (Psalm 69:26)

Taking advantage of someone at his or her most vulnerable point demonstrates the black heart of demons. To talk and gossip about a person's pain and persecute the wounded and hurting reveals the vilest lack of love, the very opposite of Jesus Christ. They are of the crowd that stood below Jesus while He hung on the cross and mocked Him to come down; like the crowd that gave Him gall and vinegar instead of love and prayers. That is why David in the Psalms, asked God to blot them out of the Book of Life.[5] Read it for yourself in the following scripture:

> Scorn has broken my heart and has left me helpless; I looked for sympathy, but there was none, for comforters, but I found none. They put gall in my food and gave me vinegar for my thirst. May the table set before them become a snare; may it become retribution and a trap. May their eyes be darkened so they cannot see, and their backs be bent forever. Pour out your wrath on them; let your fierce anger overtake them. May their place be deserted; let there be no one to dwell in their tents. For they persecute those you wound and talk about the pain of those you hurt. Charge them with crime upon crime; do not let them share in your salvation. May they be *blotted out of the Book of Life* and not be listed with the righteous. (Psalm 69:20–28, emphasis added)

Let us shudder as we contemplate in silence before the Lord the terrible outcome of those who gossip. Especially those who gossip about the gospel.

- Their table becomes a snare, a retribution and trap.
- Their eyes are darkened so they become blind.
- Their backs are bent forever in hell.
- God poured His wrath out with fierce anger.
- Their place is deserted.
- They are charged with crime upon crime.
- They are blotted out of the Book of Life.
- They fall from grace.

The last thing the Christian community needs is another cult busting group, expert, or someone's "concern." The church needs the enlightenment and love of the Holy Spirit that works rich obedience to God. This obedience by the grace of God[6] would do far more good in showing the world the truth than all the disguised gossip. Be careful that the gossip has not poisoned your mind against a church or minister. Little wonder David asked God to charge them with crime upon crime and blot them out of the Book of Life. Our prayer, like his, should be that such people do not share in God's salvation. If you have committed this sin, may you repent, for the prayers of the saints stand against you.

Poison paralyzes and often destroys completely those infected by it. It throws the body into shock, sending waves of pain through it. Those with true faith in Jesus can handle the deadly snakes who inject poison by their slander. They can pick them up in their hands and drink their poison, but it will not harm them in any way because they have learned to overcome them by an obedience that comes from faith.[7]

> . . . they will pick up snakes with their hands; and when they drink deadly poison, it will not hurt them at all; (Mark 16:18a)

As with Paul, the heat of fire or holy zeal for God will drive the viper to latch on and inject its poison, yet it will be thrown off as nothing. Throw the gossip, slander, and bitter roots back into the flames to be burned up in God's holy judgment. On the other hand, those libel for judgment, whether claiming to be Christian or not, will become infected with the vipers poison and die spiritually.

> Paul gathered a pile of brushwood and, as he put it on the fire, a viper, driven out by the heat, fastened itself on his hand. When the islanders saw the snake hanging from his hand, they said to each other, "This man must be a murderer; for though he escaped from the sea, Justice has not allowed him to live." But Paul shook the snake off into the fire and suffered no ill effects. The people expected him to swell up or suddenly fall dead, but after waiting a long time and seeing nothing unusual happen to him, they changed their minds and said he was a god. (Acts 28:3–6)

Satan, a deadly poisonous viper, defiles and kills many. Those, however, who hunger for God will build up an immunity to his poison. They can hear God's voice in spite of the viper's gossiping hiss.

CHAPTER 5

A False Witness

One of the six things God hates is a false witness who pours out lies and He detests a man who stirs up dissension among brothers. You know; things like discussion groups that talk of others and prayer groups that use prayer as a cloak for gossip.

> There are six things the Lord hates, seven that are detestable to him: haughty eyes, a lying tongue, hands that shed innocent blood, a heart that devises wicked schemes, feet that are quick to rush into evil, a false witness who pours out lies and a man who stirs up dissension among brothers. (Proverbs 6:16–19)

The key word here is "witness." They saw it. They were there. They had first-hand experience with the person in question. They were witnesses, so we believe them. Yet we need to consider the following scripture.

> A truthful witness gives honest testimony, but a false witness tells lies. (Proverbs 12:17)

So simple a statement yet so true, but unfortunately few believe it and often listen to the false witness. Let us begin to crucify self, and we will discover most men are unreliable, false witnesses.[1] This is serious because to merely listen to a false witness places your salvation in jeopardy.

> A false witness will perish, and whoever listens to him will be destroyed forever. (Proverbs 21:28)

Not only will a false witness perish, but those who listen to him will also be forever destroyed. It is of the utmost importance to our salvation that we identify a false witness and, with great effort, completely avoid them. The New Testament tells us not to even eat lunch with slanderers.[2] Unfortunately, I know pastors who sit down on a weekly basis with other pastors known to be slanderers. They do so all in the name of love, kindness, and in the spirit of working together. The only kind of "working together" this produces is an increase of sin and darkness. We can never disobey the Lord in the name of God's love and expect His approval. This is folly of an extreme nature.

Self-Serving

We listen to the false witness because self receives something out of the deal, just as Eve gained from listening to the serpent. What aspect of self is fed when you listen to a false witness? Is it self-righteousness in a cause or work?

Could it be self-justification from the conviction of the Holy Spirit? Do you want to use the insight as an excuse not to suffer persecution for Christ? Or does it make you feel more spiritual to hear about the faults of others, even if false?

Could it be that not taking the sinister advice of a gossip would upset your comfortable Christian walk? In other words, it is easier to go along with wicked men than to stand against them. Not becoming involved always feels more comfortable than standing up against a false witness. How many Christian men and women are "polluted wells" not because of what they do, but because of what they do not do? They do not resist the false witness. Don't underestimate the power of a solid, clear rebuke in the Lord, which would promote more peace and love than all the toleration the church boasts about. How sad that many pride themselves on not gossiping but quietly sit by when others do. Such nobility is a liability to Christ. Silence resembles a muddied spring or polluted well to God, something that needs a lot of clean-up before it is of any use. How many consider themselves strong in the Lord, but are polluted wells God is forced to use? These are especially the kind who reassure us that God will soon destroy all liars and not to worry about the gossip. These polluted wells of individuals, in the name of the promises of God, coldly turn away from demanding righteousness. God will judge such self-centered individuals more severely than those who spread the gossip—for they strike directly at the heart of love to kill it. This unloving crowd says, "Keep warm and well fed," but do nothing about it.

> Like a muddied spring or a polluted well is a righteous man who gives way to the wicked. (Proverbs 25:26)

Instead of giving way to the wicked why not "join with" those who suffer slander and persecution because of the cross of Christ?[3] Consider who influences you, because the people you fellowship with reflect the truth or lie you live. Those who have a hot flame of love for Jesus cannot stand a false witness. They can no more tolerate a gossiper than the sun can tolerate cold. If we cannot tell, or hear from the Lord who tells the truth, then we have a long, long way to go before we can talk about being mature in our salvation.

Guarded Love

A false witness, whether they believe what they say or not, has a goal to stop true, loving Christian fellowship between individuals. You don't have to spend time examining every argument of a false witness. Just hear from the Holy Spirit as to what lies in the heart and reject the false witness. In fact, don't bog yourself down trying to dispel every position in the discussion. You will never accomplish anything until the gossiper crucifies his heart, confesses the sin, and repents. For every time you solve one issue, a false witness will bring up another and then another. You can reach no end to the accusations of a false witness because truth is not the prize they want. Indeed, a false witness cannot stand the fact that righteous men fellowship in the truth, and so, with great effort, seek to divide relationships. If a false witness can cool your love for another in Christ they will be satisfied with that. Satan will allow a church to have sound doctrine and solid teaching, if he can keep us guarded in our love toward one another. If the false witness can make you keep an arm's length away from a true disciple of Jesus, then he wins. Therefore Paul felt thrilled to write the following to the Thessalonians. Paul knew that Satan uses many a man to cool love, fashion hate, and inflame bitter roots toward God's people. Paul probably felt shocked they had not been defiled. Whenever we are invited to speak, Satan will send someone before or after we leave to spoil the joy of the fellowship. Satan seeks desperately to whisper in someone's ear at night some negative thing that can cool the heat of godly love. Paul felt thrilled they still had pleasant memories of him, because he understood well how the Devil uses the small morsels of gossip to undermine love in the church.

> But Timothy has just now come to us from you and has brought good news about your faith and love. He has told us that you always have pleasant memories of us and that you long to see us, just as we also long to see you. Therefore, brothers, in all our distress and persecution we were encouraged about you because of your faith. (1 Thessalonians 3:6–7)

To fellowship; to love as Jesus loves, means we will have to push past every false witness, and therefore John wrote the following. The "so that" is living love that flows from the Holy Spirit and gives sound doctrine its full meaning.

> We proclaim to you what we have seen and heard, so that you also may have fellowship with us. And our

> fellowship is with the Father and with his Son, Jesus Christ. (1 John 1:3)

Unless you stand up and say, "They are brothers, true Christians I would die with and I love them," Satan, using the false witness, wins. Again, do you fellowship with those persecuted and slandered or are you taken captive by false witnesses?

Choose Sides

So many think there are two sides to every story. There is, however, only one side to any story—God's side. Consider Job for a brief moment. God pounded Job with question after question. He made Job feel like dirt. At the end of this inquisition by God, Job says, "My ears had heard of you but now my eyes have seen you. Therefore I despise myself and repent in dust and ashes."[4]

Job said many wrong things about God, and clearly saw himself as worthless and in need of much correction. No doubt Job's friends thought they made right judgments about Job. No doubt they sang "Hallelujah" in their hearts because God proved them correct. In fact, the evidence supported the side of Job's friends. After all, they *appeared* right as God spoke. But only God knows the full truth of a situation and He dealt with Job's friends. Don't wait until it is too late for God to deal with you about your "correct" judgments. Don't wait until God becomes angry as He did with Job's friends.

> After the Lord had said these things to Job, he said to Eliphaz the Temanite, "I am angry with you and your two friends, because you have not spoken of me what is right, as my servant Job has. So now take seven bulls and seven rams and go to my servant Job and sacrifice a burnt offering for yourselves. My servant Job will pray for you, and I will accept his prayer and not deal with you according to your folly. You have not spoken of me what is right, as my servant Job has." So Eliphaz the Temanite, Bildad the Shuhite and Zophar the Naamathite did what the Lord told them; and the Lord accepted Job's prayer. (Job 42:7–9)

How can a man like Job be that wrong and still be right? Easy; because the Lord said so. Job may have been wrong, had faults, wavered, struggled, slipped, sinned, and made many mistakes, but compared to his friends' sins, he had no faults at all. Only when we see our faults and sins clearly, will we see how others can be more righteous than ourselves, even when they have weaknesses. Only those who listen to God know this kind of truth in any matter. In fact, we must consider others better than ourselves.[5]

Running from Sin

Now let us look again at the word "witness." Very often someone will say, "But I was in that church. I saw things firsthand." Many show up at our church talking bad about the church they just left. Such people declare that they speak the truth. We know the possibility that they could be "false witnesses," and therefore thoroughly test what they say.[6] Some people are just fault-finders and see things wrong in everyone and everything, and must be rebuked.[7] On top of all that we all have sins that cause us to see situations wrong, and we must let God deal with these sins if we want our daily interactions with others to be truthful. We must ask God, "Are they a false witness?" To never raise the question makes us a fool of fools.

Some people alter, slur, slander, and gossip about the character of others because they have sin to hide. Are you running from sin and flesh that you haven't let God deal with? If so, you set yourself up as a prime target for a false witness or may even be a false witness yourself and not even know it. You may even dislike a ministry, not because God has said they are wrong, but because you do not want to surrender something to the Lord. Have you ever noticed that when someone doesn't like some aspect of Scripture that challenges their righteousness, he or she always attacks the person who truly lives the Scripture? This is the spirit of Cain we are warned against in Scripture.

> Do not be like Cain, who belonged to the evil one and murdered his brother. And why did he murder him? Because his own actions were evil and his brother's were righteous. (1 John 3:12)

Such people never deal with their own sins, but seek to find personal fault with a church or person. John the Baptist experienced this firsthand. The Jews and John's disciples debated "ceremonial washing," but the individuals who challenged John didn't address that issue. Instead they attacked his ministry and credibility with God. So be very careful next time you speak against a church or person. God may want to bless you[8] by convicting you of sin, but you keep running from Him and attacking the godliness of others.

> An argument developed between some of John's disciples and a certain Jew over the matter of ceremonial washing. They came to John and said to him, "Rabbi, that man who was with you on the other side of the Jordan—the one you testified about—well, he is baptizing, and everyone is going to him." (John 3:25–26)

Reliable Witnesses?

Consider that Satan witnessed God's glory in heaven. You have never seen God's glory firsthand, so does Satan have a point about God? Satan did worship in heaven and maybe God has something to hide. Satan had first-hand experience and knows things about God you know nothing about. Are you prepared to trust Satan? If not, then why do you so readily trust man?[9]

Judas ministered with Jesus for over three years. He even ate the Last Supper with Jesus. He served Jesus for years, casting out demons, preaching the good news, and staying with Jesus almost unto the cross. Maybe Judas saw something we didn't. Shall we say with sarcasm, *Too bad Judas killed himself because now we will never know his viewpoint. In fact, Judas probably killed himself from that false guilt Jesus put on him?* Maybe you would like to talk to him to hear his viewpoint on the issues? Since Satan and Judas were eyewitnesses, should we listen to their viewpoint? Should we tolerate them? You of course say, "No." Then why tolerate and listen to people who gossip, slander, and slur others? Why can you not rebuke them? In fact, how many people have you ever rebuked for gossip? None or few? How can this be?

In our blindness we think that we don't listen to false witnesses. Of course not! We never see a false witness for who he is as long as he tells us what our religious flesh wants to hear. If we want to hear it, it is truth to us. Only those who enter the prayer closet, close the door, and allow God to crucify them, shutting out the clamor of all the talk, and despising a false witness, have a chance of ever knowing the real truth. For the rebellious noisy crowd spreads their altered versions of the truth they witnessed everywhere.

Understand clearly that the only way to know the truth about a person, ministry, or event, is to love God. This love must come from a crucified life and hating your own life. We fail to understand the truth because we hold onto our sins as we protest that we belong to God. Consider the following scripture. Jesus told them they needed to repent and come to God. The crowd protested that they belonged to God and had the truth. Jesus then told them the real truth, yet they couldn't understand the truth because they hardened their hearts. Think about it; these were religious, church going, promise claiming people deaf to the truth.

> "You are doing the things your own father does." "We are not illegitimate children," they protested. "The only Father we have is God himself." Jesus said to them, "If God were your Father, you would love me, for I came from God and now am here. I have not come on my

> own; but he sent me. Why is my language not clear to you? Because you are unable to hear what I say. You belong to your father, the devil, and you want to carry out your father's desire. He was a murderer from the beginning, not holding to the truth, for there is no truth in him. When he lies, he speaks his native language, for he is a liar and the father of lies. Yet because I tell the truth, you do not believe me!" (John 8:41–45)

Unfortunately, a false witness uses the sin and self in people's character to win friends and influence other people to their cause. The false witness looks for weakness of self in the hearts of others and uses it for his or her own sinister ends. Such people use the natural sin of others to plant seeds of lies, slander, and bitter roots in our hearts. The false witness tries to find out what your flesh wants to hear and strikes the strings of those words. A false witness uses ignorance about a situation as a weapon. Seldom does anyone ever fully check out a story, in the Light and according to God's Word. A false witness knows this and relies on the laziness of man to slander those he hates. Often a person is already defiled and just seeks to prove their evil opinions and suspicions true. In fact, they give a few minutes listening to the other side of the story when they have spent hours with a false witness.

Be careful in your attempt to help, that the sin of a false witness does not overcome you. Remember it is sin to listen to a false witness, and you will never find truth by listening to a false witness and then investigating the "facts." Truth is found by hearing from the Holy Spirit what is true and rebuking the false witness before he speaks.

A false witness will change the gossip slightly as you talk with them until the truth is more closely reflected. They may even resort to saying, "That is what I meant to say," but the failure comes because the rancor still fills the choice morsel. Only now, the bitterness is in the full truth and the noblest of deeds remain laced with the acidity of sinful gossip. Satan doesn't mind defiling with the truth, in fact, he prefers it. It is for him a double bonus. Very often a false witness will use mercy as bait saying, "I am only concerned for their welfare," when all along the poison of vipers drips from their lips.

When you refuse to let the cross do its painful work,[10] you become vulnerable because the true preacher will tell you not what you want to hear, but what you need to hear. Guard yourself well and consider carefully how you listen. Remember well the following commandment and demand that others also remember it.

> You shall not give false testimony against your neighbor. (Exodus 20:16)

They call it the mob mentality, which many a sociologist studied. God, however, called it sin a long, long time ago. Within each of us resides a sinful desire to go along with the crowd, because we have a perverted desire for fellowship. This sinful nature, if not killed on the cross, causes us to pervert justice, distort stories, and align ourselves with a malicious witness.

Many times we will not even be aware that the false witness takes us in and may not feel the regrets until days later when it is too late. Think of how many times you saw individuals interviewed after a riot and they did not understand why they did what they did. Many sit in prisons because a group of individuals felt convinced that they saw someone commit a crime. Rarely is someone not swept along with the crowd.

It takes those dead to self and strong in the Holy Spirit not to follow the crowd that reaches a sinful conclusion about a person, church, or ministry. We must never side with the crowd, but only stand on the side of God.

> Do not spread false reports. Do not help a wicked man by being a malicious witness. Do not follow the crowd in doing wrong. When you give testimony in a lawsuit, do not pervert justice by siding with the crowd. (Exodus 23:1–2)

Chapter 6

Bitter Roots

The bad fruit of slurs, gossip, and slander is a bitter root. This is a salvation issue and tied to missing the grace of God. We should give full attention to what God's Word says on this matter.

The life of a true disciple in Jesus walks a rough road.[1] God leads His Son's disciples always toward the cross on the weary road of many trials and sufferings in order to enter eternal life.[2] God leads us in this world just as He led the Israelites out of Egypt into the desert. Like the Israelites, we too will feel tempted to turn bitter. The cross of Christ crucifies our flesh and, like the hot sandy deserts, is unpleasant. For this reason Scripture tells us, "See to it that no one misses the grace of God and that no bitter root grows up to cause trouble and defile many." Allow me to repeat.

> See to it that no one misses the grace of God and that no bitter root grows up to cause trouble and defile many. (Hebrews 12:15)

This defiling of many can ruin whole churches just as it ruined the whole group Moses first brought out of Egypt. Many fall away and many more stumble into temptation to complain against the leadership in a church that preaches the message of the cross. Therefore Paul warned us not to grumble.

> And do not grumble, as some of them did—and were killed by the destroying angel. (1 Corinthians 10:10)

Empowered by the Holy Spirit, true preaching will crucify the self of all members in the church. If the love that comes from the Holy Spirit is in a church, then some will feel tempted to grumble against the leadership and other members of the church. Gossip provides one means by which grumbling and bitter roots spread throughout the church. Faultfinders grumble over doctrine, church projects, or the color of a tie—but it is still sinful grumbling. Even those with good hearts must remember that an undeserved curse does not rest, but will keep fluttering around and darting here and there until it finds some place to rest. Our ill spoken words do not just stop when we shut our lips.

> Like a fluttering sparrow or a darting swallow, an undeserved curse does not come to rest. (Proverbs 26:2)

Let us be very careful that we do not say to ourselves, "Oh, they deserved the curse." No man can be innocently cursed on our part unless we allow the Holy Spirit to express His very words through us. We should never open our mouths until the Holy Spirit tells us. This is what Jesus meant when He said we should not judge.[3]

The Growth of Bitter Roots

Think of roots and how they grow quietly, underground in darkness, and undetected until its ugly fruit manifests. Or signs of it start to materialize as things begin to mysteriously die and for some unknown reason a church starts to fail. Roots find any dark corner or crevice and can weave an underground web for many feet. If more than one plant spreads bitter roots they begin to intertwine and interconnect. To attempt to pull up one bitter root becomes an impossible situation because it affects every plant. If such entanglement goes on long enough the whole ground must be plowed under, giving the roots time to die so that things can grow again. The only recourse is for God to sift, split the church, or let it die.

Most importantly, how does a bitter root start? From a small seed. It doesn't take much to start a bitter root growing. A negative opinion voiced or a careless grumbling comment about the high demands of the cross often plants the seed of a bitter root. A hostile attitude about something someone said, a correction given, or in the course of normal loving fellowship, a misunderstanding occurring can cause a bitter root. Speak a little off tone and offend someone and a bitter root may start instead of covering the situation with mercy.

The Blame Game

Of course God is too big to strike at, so the person with the bitter root attacks the church and its leaders. This happened to Moses time after time until God could not allow the people into the Promised Land. Too many instances occurred of the Israelites grumbling to mention here, but one is worth quoting.[4] The people fell under judgment because of their sin. God righteously judged them, but who did they blame the next morning for the trouble? They blamed Moses and Aaron, of course! Those having a bitter root in their hearts always take things way out of proportion. They accused Moses of murder! Those filled with such bitterness will make what they experienced in a church seem like the most sinister, vile, deadly, overshadowing, and personally damaging thing they have ever experienced. They refuse to admit that it was their fault. Yes, technically Moses did bring them out to the desert and yes, because of Moses some were killed—but how backward the charge of guilt.

> The next day the whole Israelite community grumbled against Moses and Aaron. "You have killed the Lord's people," they said. (Numbers 16:41)

In short, they never humbled themselves, and admitted their sins, but instead grumbled in their tents against the leadership. Again, take note, they sinned, but blamed Moses and accused him of having bad motives.

The bitter root manifested itself by people grumbling about salvation! One reason we don't see this much today in the church is that most teachers preach a wide gate and wide road salvation call—and no one grumbles against that.

> They said to Moses, "Was it because there were no graves in Egypt that you brought us to the desert to die? What have you done to us by bringing us out of Egypt?" (Exodus 14:11)

Again, note how the Israelites exaggerated what they experienced in the "church" compared to the peace they once enjoyed. They cried, "We sat around pots of meat and ate all the food we wanted." How quickly those with bitter roots betray the church and forget they were slaves in sin.

> The Israelites said to them, "If only we had died by the Lord's hand in Egypt! There we sat around pots of meat and ate all the food we wanted, but you have brought us out into this desert to starve this entire assembly to death." (Exodus 16:3)

I once pastored a church like this that blamed me for the good news of Jesus Christ—as if it were a bad thing. Even now many who have been preached to are really grumblers with bitter roots about the salvation message of God. Everyone wants to live in the Promised Land, but very few want to carry their cross on the way. And when the road grows narrow, many grumble against leadership, look for other churches, and eagerly seek out those who will be bitter with them.

Just imagine how much worse it would have been for Moses if the Israelites had access to the Internet. With a laptop in his or her tent, they could have readily spread their bitterness throughout the camp and the world. Just think of what you would find if you had researched Moses to see if he was a true preacher of God. The odds would have easily ran a 1,000,000 to 1 against Moses. Remember, all but two perished in the desert because the Israelites grumbled against the salvation of the Lord, the grumbling focused on Moses and Aaron. When you consider how many message boards they could fill up, it staggers the mind. Today, you can easily find many more people who grumble, gossip, and spread their bitter roots against the salvation of God. Many a camp that "belongs to the Lord" spreads gossip against the gospel, just as the Israelites grumbled against the saving grace of God.

It is not hard to imagine the booksellers and authors peddling their goods of grumbling as they trod through the desert. Titles like, *The Subtle Power of Moses' Spiritual Abuse*, *Moses, the Authority Abuser,* and *The Moses Cult* could fill the bookshelves. Story after story, chapter after chapter of true life experiences from those who suffered under the leadership of Moses could have been written. Just think of how the grumbling incident could have produced over a 100,000 different true life stories of the trouble Moses' leadership brought each person.

One can only praise God the desert did not have a wireless network or publishing house. For, if the Israelites had today's means of communication, we would today suffer under a barrage of whining books about the terrible leadership of Moses and the abuse he inflicted. Such things would falsely declare that the Israelite's misery was the fault of Moses, trying to prove the gossip about him true. Praise God we do not have to carry that heavy load, but woe to us today who are overrun by modern day tell-all (at least in their own minds) whiners who refuse to take responsibility for their own sins. Woe to us because it is very hard to silence their talk long enough to hear the good news of Jesus.

It is not uncommon to find whole churches or groups whining about the manna God provides for them to eat, calling it "miserable food." Woe to those who call the offensive message of the cross "miserable food."

> . . . they spoke against God and against Moses, and said, "Why have you brought us up out of Egypt to die in the desert? There is no bread! There is no water! And we detest this miserable food!" (Numbers 21:5)

The Sound of Wailing

The church I pastored would never consider the message of the cross to be a festival in the Lord.[5] They, day in and day out, whined about the cross and found fault with anything they could with the leadership, refusing to obey with a full heart by the power of the Holy Spirit.

Like the Israelites, God time after time showed these people they grumbled. They would confess it as sin, only to return to it with a renewed vengeance later. Finally, this church destroyed itself just as the first generation of Israelites did with Moses. Such wailing in our homes fertilizes a bitter root. Whenever gossipers hear this whining they come running with their evil suspicions, slander, and slurs until they firmly plant a bitter root in the heart of those grumbling. What a scene this must have been for Moses to behold. Hundreds of people standing at the door of their tents wailing because they had been saved and must now carry their cross. Woe unto a church that considers the good news of Jesus salvation by works.

> Moses heard the people of every family wailing, each at the entrance to his tent. The Lord became exceedingly angry, and Moses was troubled. (Numbers 11:10)

Even the best of leadership will make mistakes in doing God's will. If we tolerate gossip and pass off slurs as something inoffensive, great destruction in a church will take place. Satan can have a field day with such a church, enjoying every grumble as if a sweet hymn. Satan, and those of like mind, considers gossip and grumbling as music to the ears. They eagerly grab and hunger for any news they can twist and use to support their grumbling.

The Next Generation

The second generation of Israelites learned their lessons. They saw what happened to their forefathers when they grumbled and they had no desire to commit the same sin. When Joshua and the leadership made the mistake of making a treaty with people they should not have, the Israelites "grumbled against the leaders." This generation, however, knew what happens when grumbling continues, so they pressed on in their faith in a God that would work all things for the good.[6] They didn't run off and find a different leader, because they knew their forefathers had done that and wound up sinning with a golden calf. They saw what happens to people who grumble; they saw their own faults and understood how hard it is to be a leader for God, so in compassion, quickly showed mercy toward Joshua. It wasn't that Joshua didn't allow the congregation to voice their complaints, but they did it in faith before God with fear and trembling. That is why we read nothing of judgment by God, such as a plague like their forefathers experienced. Instead, we read of Joshua and the Israelites marching into the Promised Land and winning battle after battle.

> So the Israelites set out and on the third day came to their cities: Gibeon, Kephirah, Beeroth and Kiriath Jearim. But the Israelites did not attack them, because the leaders of the assembly had sworn an oath to them by the Lord, the God of Israel. The whole assembly grumbled against the leaders, but all the leaders answered, "We have given them our oath by the Lord, the God of Israel, and we cannot touch them now." (Joshua 9:17–19)

Do not listen to those who can point out errors or sins of church leaders if it comes from their own grumblings against the cross of Christ. Now, as Hebrews 13:18 demonstrates, I am not talking about gross immorality or worldly leadership that fills the pulpit today, but of those who desire to honestly pick up their cross and follow Christ. A congregation should submit to the authority of such leaders, for there you will find "no advantage" in grumbling or gossiping about godly leadership.

> Obey your leaders and submit to their authority. They keep watch over you as men who must give an account. Obey them so that their work will be a joy, not a burden, for that would be of no advantage to you. Pray for us.

> We are sure that we have a clear conscience and desire to live honorably in every way. (Hebrews 13:17–18)

In fact, such gossip only becomes a self-fulfilling prophecy. Suppose a few start grumbling and that spreads to the rest of the body. The congregation then becomes weak, bitter roots grow, and soon the whole church turns sickly, sapping nutrients out of the church. Those who first started the gossip can say, "See, I told you the church and leadership were in bad shape." All the while, the same people blindly have no clue that they caused the destruction.

Cursing Leadership

A person makes a terrible mistake judging leadership by the behavior of the congregation. You can have the best godly leadership that God can provide and if the congregation does not want to accept the message of the cross it makes no difference. Every time God leads such a church to a new area to bless them by crucifying self, they turn the blessing into a curse.[7]

This is why there is some truth when people grumble. They had a bitter experience, but of their own making—not the fault of leadership. Though the leadership led in the way of God's will, and the advice came from the Holy Spirit, their attitude and stubborn hearts turned it into something bitter. In short, every blessing of God's guidance only worked more spiritual destruction because they had a bitter root.

This is exactly why God keeps so many in dead or unspiritual churches—they are not ready for true godly leadership. How many people complain that they can't find a good church to attend anywhere but would reject it if God pointed the way? Many whine about the corruption of today's church and complain that they can find no where to worship, when all the while the problem lies with them. For God promises that at the right time, when we become truly humble and teachable, then our teachers will be "hidden no more."

> Although the Lord gives you the bread of adversity and the water of affliction, your teachers will be hidden no more; with your own eyes you will see them. (Isaiah 30:20)

Therefore, opinionated, fault-finding grumblers cannot expect God to show them good teachers, because they would only cause a bitter root to grow. If you are a selfish believer who whines about your needs not being met, and how leadership always fails you, then don't expect God to show you His true teachers. If you remain unwilling to give up all to follow Jesus, you will certainly be unwilling to move to a church with godly leadership. So why should God guide you? If you like to grumble by saying, "There are no perfect churches," God will not give you a church that aims for perfection.[8] Indeed, you will only find the evil you look for until you are ready to die to your sins.

Destroying Bitter Roots

I have learned a hard lesson; bitter roots cannot be tolerated in any fashion. Even if someone asks good questions, but asks with even a seed of a bitter root, it must be pulled up and destroyed first *before* answering the question. Though any godly leader would rejoice in a church full of the peace of the Holy Spirit, the bitter root must be dealt with first in great power and authority.[9] Everything must stop! I do mean everything. You can't discuss any issue, pray about anything, evangelize, serve, worship, or take one step forward in God's will until the bitter root is stopped dead. Those in a church with a bitter root who ignore this advice will suffer greatly down the road because that bitterness will soon cause trouble and defile many. The camp cannot "move on" until the congregation is cleansed and repents of the bitter root.

> So Miriam was confined outside the camp for seven days, and the people did not move on till she was brought back. (Numbers 12:15)

You can't build a faithful church with bitter roots present—not even with the seed of a bitter root. This is why Paul wrote that the Corinthians would not find him as they wanted him to be.

> For I am afraid that when I come I may not find you as I want you to be, and you may not find me as you want me to be. I fear that there may be quarreling, jealousy, outbursts of anger, factions, slander, gossip, arrogance and disorder. (2 Corinthians 12:20)

Once grumbling gossip spreads a bitter root, it first overgrows the issue at hand, but soon overtakes every aspect of a church. As the overgrowth of a bitter root chokes out and weaves its way into each person's heart, the love of the Holy Spirit dies. Indeed, all in the name of the love of God, members begin to bite at each other, until finally devouring everyone and completely spiritually destroying the church.

> If you keep on biting and devouring each other, watch out or you will be destroyed by each other. (Galatians 5:15)

Take a Stand

Avoid, like the plague, anyone with an ax to grind, who hides in darkness and overflows with bitterness. Only those who stand up to the sin of bitter roots will stop the judgment of God. On the other hand, those who refuse to take a stand against the sin will easily be swept away. As you read the following scripture, notice Aaron stopped the Lord's wrath, caused from grumbling, because he stood up—but not before God destroyed 14,700 people. If Aaron had not stood up God would have put an end to the Israelites "at once." Eventually they totally wasted all of Moses' intercession and wandered and died in the desert of Sin. Indeed they were denied entrance into the Promise Land. Those who do not give up their bitterness will never experience the joy of the crucified life.

> But when the assembly gathered in opposition to Moses and Aaron and turned toward the Tent of Meeting, suddenly the cloud covered it and the glory of the Lord appeared. Then Moses and Aaron went to the front of the Tent of Meeting, and the Lord said to Moses, "Get away from this assembly so I can put an end to them at once." And they fell facedown. Then Moses said to Aaron, "Take

> your censer and put incense in it, along with fire from the altar, and hurry to the assembly to make atonement for them. Wrath has come out from the Lord; the plague has started." So Aaron did as Moses said, and ran into the midst of the assembly. The plague had already started among the people, but Aaron offered the incense and made atonement for them. He stood between the living and the dead, and the plague stopped. But 14,700 people died from the plague, in addition to those who had died because of Korah. (Numbers 16:42–49)

Are you willing to take a stand against bitter roots perhaps breeding in your study group, discussion group, or neighborhood—or even in your own heart? If so, it will cost your comfort and much of yourself because only fire from the altar will make the incense of prayer acceptable to God. No laid back attitude or discussion with a bitter person will stop the plague and judgment of God. It calls for the utmost in urgency, zeal, and sacrifice of self to cause God to hold back His judgment.

As stated before, I have seen a church suffer under the judgment of God because they grumbled against the message of the cross. In this church, no one stood up to the judgment and instead, one by one, defiled each other with their grumbling and bitter roots. Oh, like Moses, I interceded before God, but found no Aaron to stand up in the assembly. To God's glory, however, I have also witnessed a church where members stand up to bitter roots and stop the plague of sin from spreading throughout the church. I cannot express to you the difference between the sheer pain of one and the supreme joy of the other. There is nothing like the oil of the Holy Spirit that permits a church to fellowship in the love of God no matter how hard the cross comes against sin. Such fellowship is indeed, "precious oil," like that running down on the beard of Aaron. The same Aaron we previously read about, who did not grumble with bitterness against Moses, but lifted up a censor of prayer that stopped the sin. How precious are such men in God's sight, approved not only by Him, but by man as well. Those who lift the censor of prayer against bitter roots and wrestle gossip down before God will sing the song of ascents. Such people can move closer to God.

> A song of ascents. Of David. How good and pleasant it is when brothers live together in unity! It is like precious oil poured on the head, running down on the beard, running down on Aaron's beard, down upon the collar of his robes. (Psalm 133:1–2)

CHAPTER 7

Betrayers and Parent Cursers

Up until now we merely hinted at the worst type of sin. Now let's take a straight look at the gossip of those who betray; the top of the class in terms of gossipers. This type of gossiper betrays their parents or those they once fellowshipped with in the Lord. They commit the sin of Judas but do not have the courtesy to hang themselves. Betrayal is the most corrupt and contemptible form of gossip that comes from one who betrays love, fellowship, and intimacy. The sting of their sin is like no other form of gossip. Even Jesus felt appalled that Judas betrayed Him with a kiss.

Like the trapping of a defenseless animal for sport, the very nature of this kind of gossip forces its victims into a most appalling corner. These betrayers use the most intimate of information to spread their gossip. Indeed, their closeness to the ones they betray gives them an air of authority and respectability, an opportunity to speak information unavailable to anyone else. And when you defend yourself with the truth, you must discuss the most personal of information. This is why David wrote a prayer in the form of a song in Psalm 55

It is relatively easy to endure the gossip spat by enemies of the cross, but when those we loved by the Holy Spirit betray our open and vulnerable love, the pain wrenches the soul. Those who once enjoyed sweet fellowship in the church, yet betrayed their families and friends, have the most serious of sins to repent of. Such sin is not easily atoned for.[1] These people use their past fellowship as a tool to justify their current sinfulness. Remember, if we cannot win our case with the truth, without slandering others, then we have no case. Our cause is a lie, a darkness called light. All we need do is look at the bad fruit of such gossipers. He betrayed a fellow man. In other words, he demands more of the man he gossips about than himself. He betrays a "close friend" with whom he used to joyfully walk to church. We considered this person a special friend among the "throng" of people that massed themselves together to worship the Lord; a friend we could pick out of a crowd and for which our hearts leapt for joy. This is the kind of friend that became a foe.

> If an enemy were insulting me, I could endure it; if a foe were raising himself against me, I could hide from him. But it is you, a man like myself, my companion, my close friend, with whom I once enjoyed sweet fellowship as we walked with the throng at the house of God. (Psalms 55:12–14)

Parent Cursers

Today many people commonly complain against their parents, to curse their names, and speak evil with malicious intent. Such people use their parents to justify their own problems and sins. They use closeness of family life and the personal information as a weapon of warfare to win the battle in justifying their lives of sin. After all, no matter what kind of family life a person grew up under, if they cry out to God, their godliness and righteousness would far outshine any complaints. As Proverbs tells us, such individuals will have their lamps snuffed out with darkness quickly overtaking them.

> If a man curses his father or mother, his lamp will be snuffed out in pitch darkness. (Proverbs 20:20)

We each stand accountable only before God, and the supposed vileness of another will by no means justify us before a holy God. The Lord made this clear when He stated that those who curse their parents would find their blood on their "own head(s)."

> If anyone curses his father or mother, he must be put to death. He has cursed his father or his mother, and his blood will be on his own head. (Leviticus 20:9)

If you hear anyone using their father or mother, cursing them by blaming them for their problems, or telling tales or speaking ill of them, you had best move to the other side of the camp as quickly as possible. For their judgment and wrath will come soon enough and you do not want to be swept away with them. This is why I tell children whose parents have left the faith to stay quiet about the matter. Let others speak of their sins when required, but the son or daughter should remain as silent as possible.

The First Gossip

Consider the first instance of family gossip mentioned in the Bible—Noah and his sons. Noah, a mighty man of God, a man of persevering faith and obedience to the will of God, saved his family, but became drunk one day. Not your everyday kind of drunknness, but passed out.

> The sons of Noah who came out of the ark were Shem, Ham and Japheth. (Ham was the father of Canaan.) These were the three sons of Noah, and from them came the people who were scattered over the earth. Noah, a man of the soil, proceeded to plant a vineyard. When he drank some of its wine, he became drunk and lay uncovered inside his tent. (Genesis 9:18–21)

Noah labored for hundreds of years building the Ark which saved his sons, Shem, Ham, and Japheth, from God's judgment. God placed Noah in charge of the Ark to care for all the animals. To say the least, Noah must have felt worn out from the work. No doubt out of weariness he became drunk and lay uncovered in his tent. Ham was the first to walk in on the situation and like a little school girl went out to the playground to tattle-tale on his father. You can easily imagine him whispering to his other brothers, with a slight giggle in his voice, about their father's drunkenness and nakedness. In short, this was the first incident recorded in the Bible of someone gossiping.

> Ham, the father of Canaan, saw his father's nakedness and told his two brothers outside. (Genesis 9:22)

Let us understand we are not talking about ignoring gross immorality in a family. Such families need to be called to repentance. Rather, we must consider the whole man when we see faults and sins. There is no doubt God approved of Noah, therefore Ham's reaction came from a heart of shaming gossip and slander. The other two brothers had a love and respect for their father. Shem and Japheth refused to inquire any further in the matter, but turned their backs to this fault in Noah. They walked backwards into the tent and covered their father's sin. In fact, they went to great lengths to place a blanket over their shoulders and walk backwards to make sure they did not humiliate Noah. As Scripture records this good deed, "their faces were turned the other way." They refused to even look at the sin because they had the heart of godly love that could easily see the heart of Noah. They knew that God's grace would overcome this relapse into sin. They had not forgotten that Noah was a man of obedient faith and knew this would not be his life's pattern. If Ham would have been alive today he would have, with great speed, contacted any number of Christian magazines, called others, e-mailed friends, and logged onto any number of message groups.

> But Shem and Japheth took a garment and laid it across their shoulders; then they walked in backward and covered their father's nakedness. Their faces were turned the other way so that they would not see their father's nakedness. (Genesis 9:23)

A Wicked Son

Shem and Japheth covered over their father's sin, unlike David's son, Absalom, who spread gossip far and wide for his own selfish ends. Although David sinned, we must note it was *David* who sinned. David, who had been forgiven by God for the adultery and conspiracy to cover his evil; David, who God disciplined; David who God said was after His own heart. For Absalom and others to use gossip in a time of David's weakness and discipline reveals a blackened heart of hatred and selfishness. There can be little doubt that Absalom probably justified himself by thinking that his father wasn't all that righteous. I don't know about you, reader, but I would rather follow a David on the run under God's discipline than help an Absalom use gossip to gain power. Woe unto those who curse their father and mother!

> Ahithophel answered, "Lie with your father's concubines whom he left to take care of the palace. Then all Israel will hear that you have made yourself a stench in your father's nostrils, and the hands of everyone with you will be strengthened." So they pitched a tent for Absalom on the roof, and he lay with his father's concubines in the sight of all Israel. (2 Samuel 16:21–22)

"All Israel will hear," was Absalom's goal. He used gossip as a means to achieve his personal agenda and solidify current wicked friendships. Like Absalom, many a son or daughter has ridiculed their parents to their friends. That form of family gossip occurs all too commonly throughout the teen years, for such poison of vipers rests on all men's lips. But when a son or daughter spreads gossip against those he or she grew up with in a godly home, God's anger must burn doubly hot.

A Holy Covenant

When we fellowship with others by the love of Jesus, or call someone brother or sister, we make a covenant with them. In doing so, we state directly that we will lay down our lives for them and, like Jesus, will never leave or forsake them. Such covenants are holy in nature and binding because they are commitments based on God's love. Such covenants tell others that they may open up to us the most personal of information, struggles, and vulnerabilities, and that such matters remain safe with us. Just as when we pray before God and pour out our hearts, our lives, and our sins in the safety of Christ's love, that is what a brother or sister tells us when they worship with us at church. No more would it enter our minds that Jesus would take personal information and share it with wicked men simply for the sake of His own pleasure, should we ever expect such behavior from men who have made a covenant of love with us. When we confess our sins to one another as Scripture demands, and then someone betrays that confession—well, there are not enough words to describe such a vile betrayal!

Like Jesus, we in the church are called to remain faithful toward one another; no matter what sins we think someone may have. One can't help but think of Jonathan who died on the battlefield with unfaithful Saul rather than betray the commitment to his father. What an encouragement it is to look at Jonathan who managed to uphold righteousness through his love of David, while at the same time not break faith with his father.

Those who betray in this class violate holiness, the character of God, itself.

> My companion attacks his friends; he violates his covenant. (Psalms 55:20)

Smooth Talkers

This form of gossip often seems as smooth as butter and as soothing as oil. This gossip does not always occur with the outward vengeance an enemy must use. Because the intimate knowledge of personal information affords a more sinister method of attack, a smooth tactic may be applied. These betrayers can speak of concern, of love, and a desire for the truth of Jesus to be revealed. Their method of war is with the weapon of kindness.

> His speech is smooth as butter, yet war is in his heart; his words are more soothing than oil, yet they are drawn swords. (Psalms 55:21)

To spot these kind of gossipers do not look for direct malice in their speech, but for kind words laced with bitterness. The key they use to the door of your heart is like butter and oil. Once you unlatch the lock to gossip and it enters in, they draw the sword to kill truth and love. Be not fooled by the fact they were once friends with those they speak against. Instead let it be a warning to you. If such people willingly betray the most personal of friends, will they not likewise betray you at an opportune time? If nothing else, you should be wise enough to know that if they treat others this way, they will react with the same wickedness toward you if you do not serve them well. In short, if you listen to a friend tell you tales about an ex-friend—you would be stupid to befriend them or share anything from your own life.

Destruction

Let it be a further warning that God will send all such gossipers into a pit of corruption.

> But you, O God, will bring down the wicked into the pit of corruption; bloodthirsty and deceitful men will not live out half their days. But as for me, I trust in you. (Psalms 55:23)

A pit of corruption. Who can fully contemplate what this means? In such a place, truth is corrupted with a slight twist of lies over and over again for all eternity. In the end, all betrayers will gather into one place to voice their tales and stories in the torment of hell. God will place those who spoke with the smoothness of oil, but yet were bloodthirsty, in a pit with others of like heart. Those who love the Lord will be rewarded with the image of Christ, while the betrayer class will be chained together for all eternity with others who reflect their own darkness.

Amazingly, in claiming the charity of Jesus such wicked people betray with calculated vengeance. They continue to prowl the city, the Internet, the church, or the neighborhood; never satisfied until they destroy all goodness and justify their lies.

> Day and night they prowl about on its walls; malice and abuse are within it. Destructive forces are at work in the city; threats and lies never leave its streets. (Psalms 55:10–11)

In the churches I have pastored the love of Christ has always manifested itself powerfully. The joy that comes from walking in the Light and hating our lives for Christ causes the love of God to burst forth into some of the deepest fellowship that one can have this side of heaven. But it also makes us extremely vulnerable to those who turn their backs on God and set out to gossip. For when they leave they have tools of wickedness that should never be used by any man.

The Spirit of Cain

Betrayers slander because if the righteous are justified by God, then the gossipers are dead wrong. They must slander in order to justify themselves to their families and other men. Their bad consciences allow them no rest until they become so corrupted that they believe the lies declared.

Like Cain, they desperately want to believe their lies and slander. For this reason John wrote a short letter of warning for any Christian to not become a Cain. A Cain attacks another brother or sister because his or her life is more righteous than his.

> Do not be like Cain, who belonged to the evil one and murdered his brother. And why did he murder him? Because his own actions were evil and his brother's were righteous. (1 John 3:12)

We must never forget the Old Testament story about Cain. If a Cain invites you into his field to talk about another, or to worship or fellowship, do not go! For he will strike with gossip to kill others or strike with violence if the opportunity presents itself. Much of the gossip in the Christian community results purely from the vile spirit of Cain. Be very careful that you are not drawn into this sin by tolerating such men or women.

Trust the Lord

When faced with such betrayal from children or friends there is only one thing to do. We must do what Jesus did on the cross as they crucified Him, naked and vulnerable. He trusted God. It is easy to become unsettled by such mean-spirited attacks, to act out of fretting or hatred, but let me encourage the reader to do what I have learned, run to God in prayer and trust Him. For soon enough, if the gossipers do not repent, they will enter hell in a most miserable way and be assigned a place we would not want to even contemplate in our nightmares. We must say with David, and countless saints who have faced the betrayal and cursing of men, *But as for me, I trust in you* (Psalm 55:23).

Chapter 8

Sinfully Rich Morsels

Proverbs tells us that gossip is like no other dish or food we eat. When a man eats a meal it merely enters his body and leaves it at a later time. The joy of the food lasts but a few moments as each bite rests on the tongue and is then swallowed and digested. Gossip is not like that, it is a choice meal where even a small morsel becomes a treasured treat. Gossip enters a man and goes all the way into his heart, passing through his spirit, and finally resting in his soul.

> The words of a gossip are like choice morsels; they go down to a man's inmost parts. (Proverbs 26:22)

Begin to tell someone a tad bit of gossip and they will stop and give you their full attention. Start your sentence with, "*Did you hear?*" and you will have the attention of the world.

Since gossip is a sinful food we enjoy eating, we find much joy in cooking up such a meal. We savor each ingredient, every bit of news, and stir with great delight before we bake it in the heat of our sinful ovens.

Very often gossip grows way out of proportion to what actually took place, because we cook a story over and over. As a pastor of Christ, many stories have been spread about me, some of them funny, even outlandish, and still others threatening, but none of them innocent before the Lord. For example, we just heard the other day, (I trust the reader will catch the phrase) that an unnamed person told someone that I married my wife by taking over a church, kicking out her husband, and sweeping her off to be my bride. Of course there exists a kernel of truth to the story—I *am* married to my wife. However, many of the stories about our ministry have absolutely *no* truth to them. Everything else in this particular tale, for example, is a lie—and the person who told the story should have been rebuked and brought out into the Light. Indeed, if the gossiper felt it important enough to tell someone else, then he or she should have called us first. These are the very basics of Christian love and charity.

Let me set the record straight before pressing on. Neither my wife, nor I, have been married before. I was nineteen and she was eighteen when we married nearly thirty years ago. I did not even become a Christian until several years later.

A Recipe for Sin

There are normal choice morsels of gossip and then there are the *sinfully rich* choice morsels. One is your average talk of the town, while the other comes from a false witness, faultfinder, and most vile of all, the betrayer. The following recipe is for *Sinfully Rich Choice Morsels*, a betrayer's favorite food.

Before you read the recipe on the next page, consider the term morsel. Scripture calls gossip choice morsels; particular pieces of information, selecting just what to say, how to say it, and what should be digested more than other parts of information. Just as we buy select pieces of meat, a choice morsel is a very select, juicy piece of gossip. These extremely small pieces of food excite our entire being. The ears eagerly listen for the news of a morsel, the eyes excitedly scan to see the morsel, the hands eagerly pick up and feel the texture, while the tongue savors the various exotic flavors. The heart ravenously picks up on the aroma of a possible piece of news, the spirit zealously obtains more information and the soul only feels satisfied when the morsel reaches the inmost part of a person. The nugget may seem a small thing that we consider an insignificant sin, but it turns our life to heaven or hell. As James wrote;

> Or take ships as an example. Although they are so large and are driven by strong winds, they are steered by a very small rudder wherever the pilot wants to go. Likewise the tongue is a small part of the body, but it makes great boasts. Consider what a great forest is set on fire by a small spark. (James 3:4-5)

Finally, forests are set on fire by a spark and our whole being is turned to darkness by a small morsel called gossip. (You can obtain a poster of the following recipe at www.morsels.org.)

Sinfully Rich Choice Morsels

Ingredients

1 cup pride —Proverbs 21:24
3/4 cup hearsay —Ephesians 4:29
1/2 cup evil suspicions —1 Timothy 6:3–4
1/4 cup grumbling —1 Corinthians 10:10
1 tablespoon bitterness —Ephesians 4:29
3/4 tablespoon slander —Leviticus 19:16
2 teaspoons yeast of exaggeration —1 Corinthians 5:8
3 teaspoons of slurring the situation —Psalm 15:3
Pinch of flattery —Jude :16
Just a dash of unfaithfulness to Jesus —John 6:66

Directions

1. Mix together all ingredients in a bowl of betrayal. —Proverbs 16:28; Matthew 26:23
2. Pour into a medium saucepan and bring to a boil; constantly stirring. —Proverbs 6:14
3. Prepare in a dark kitchen. —John 3:20
4. Turn on low and simmer overnight. —Ephesians 4:26–27
5. Sprinkle with the truth (optional). —Romans 1:25
6. Serve hot to itching ears, warm to those not minding their own business, and cold to those fearful. —Acts 14:2; 1 Thessalonians 4:11; 2 Timothy 4:3

Makes Unlimited Servings —Proverbs 4:24; 1 Timothy 1:6

www.morsels.org

Spreading Gossip

Once a woman came to us under deep conviction about the gossip she spread around the town where I pastor. She felt offended by the message of the cross and in order to justify herself, embittered everyone she could find. A year or so later she hurt sorely over the crimes she had committed. She came to our house, sat in the living room and wept over what she did. She asked for forgiveness, which we gave. This woman later, however, refused to put in writing or confess to the people she defiled that she had been wrong about the lies she spread. While we forgave her, God does not forgive such self-centered repentance. She only had worldly sorrow, and like many slanderous past members, was filled with regret at ever having "repented."

> Godly sorrow brings repentance that leads to salvation and leaves no regret, but worldly sorrow brings death. (2 Corinthians 7:10)

Indeed, sad to say, our act of kindness will be nothing but heaping coals of burning sulfur poured on her head when God finally judges her sin.

Let me share with you an anonymous story I found, which I then ran in a local newspaper entitled, "Chicken Feathers."

Chicken Feathers

> A middle-aged pastor in a small farming community in the Midwest had been falsely accused. It was a vicious, scandalous story, and it swept through town like a prairie fire.

"Have your heard about the pastor?"

"Can you believe it?"

"He ought to leave town."

"You'd never think such a thing to look at him, would you?"

"Guess he had a lot of us fooled."

"His poor wife."

After a period of time, however, the rumor was found to be just that . . . an ugly, empty rumor, without any basis in fact. But the damage had already been done. Many people in the town had believed every word and were now reluctant to revise their opinions.

("There must have been some truth in it, or why would everybody be talking about it?")

Some time later, the couple who had spread the false tale came under conviction of sin and went to the pastor to apologize. Confessing they had known the rumor to be false all along, they asked the offended man for forgiveness.

"Of course I will forgive you," he replied gravely. "But could I ask you to do something for me? Something that might seem rather strange at first?" Relieved that the pastor was willing to forgive, the couple readily agreed to do whatever he asked.

"All right," he said, "here is my request. I would like you to go home and butcher one of your chickens, pluck out all its feathers, and put the feathers in a bag. Could you do that for me?"

They nodded yes; they could certainly do that. But it seemed so strange. Was the man asking for a chicken?

"Next," the pastor went on, "I'd like you to go through town and at each corner, scatter some of the feathers—just a few—from the bag. Then, please take the remaining feathers and climb to the top of the old city water tower—you know, the one by the feed store—and scatter those to the wind. Could you do those things?"

They were mystified by the point but nodded in the affirmative once again.

"Fine," the pastor said, "just fine." The couple stood up to leave. But as they reached the door, he suddenly called them back. "Oh. There's just one more thing, please. After you've finished scattering all the feathers, I'd just like you to go back through town and gather them all up again. Okay? Make sure that you pick up every one you've dropped and every one you've scattered to the winds, and put them all back in the bag. Please be careful that none of the feathers are missing, and bring them back to me. Could you do that for me?"

The couple just stared at him. "Pastor, that's impossible," the man said. "The wind will have blown them all over three counties by then."

The pastor didn't say a word, and slowly the truth of his word picture began to dawn on the couple, and they hung their heads. Yes, they could be forgiven for their actions, but no one could undo the damage they had done by scattering their false and slanderous words.

Without wood a fire goes out; without gossip a quarrel dies down. (Proverbs 26:20)

In over twenty years of preaching in different parts of the world, gossip and bitter roots always create problems. As individuals encounter things they do not understand or our teaching reveals hidden sins, gossip often bursts forth. As the Proverb declares, without gossip a quarrel ceases. It is acceptable to disagree with an individual or doctrine, but we should never resort to gossip to prove our point, or use bitter roots to win the day, because in so doing we may miss the grace of God. He will condemn us for causing a bitter root to grow in someone else. Remember, it will take a whole church to "see to it" that no bitter root grows and that no one misses the grace of God. It will take the prayers, wisdom, and the Holy Spirit in each person to "see to it" that bitter roots never take root. Let me repeat the scripture.

> See to it that no one misses the grace of God and that no bitter root grows up to cause trouble and defile many. (Hebrews 12:15)

Chapter 9

Look in the Mirror

Let's take time to be honest about what we look like; to take a long, slow, clear look at ourselves in the mirror. Below I quote James 1:23 all the way to verse 26 to make a point. James tells us to look intently, no casual glance here, into the perfect law of Christ—the law of love. And in verse 26 the very first thing James asks us to reflect upon is our tongue.

> Anyone who listens to the word but does not do what it says is like a man who looks at his face in a mirror and, after looking at himself, goes away and immediately forgets what he looks like. But the man who looks intently into the perfect law that gives freedom, and continues to do this, not forgetting what he has heard, but doing it— he will be blessed in what he does. If anyone considers himself religious and yet does not keep a tight rein on his tongue, he deceives himself and his religion is worthless. (James 1:23–26)

We need to be honest with ourselves; if our religion is worthless because of our tongue then now is the time to joyfully repent. For example, as you prepare for church on Sundays, do you sober yourself up taking a renewed look at your conversation and the need to shut up as you enter through the doors of the church? Examine in what manner your steps take you to church. Look at each step carefully to make sure it is full of the Holy Spirit so God will place a guard over your mouth. By working our salvation out with fear and trembling, we can surrender our conversations to the Lord.

> Set a guard over my mouth, O Lord; keep watch over the door of my lips. (Psalm 141:3)

Not only will the Holy Spirit purify our talk, but a blessed silence and peace will enter our lives. Most of us talk too much for God to take us into His confidence. For the Lord knows that if He shared any more of Himself with us, we would blab it all over the place. Therefore God admonishes us to avoid those who talk "too much."

> A gossip betrays a confidence; so avoid a man who talks too much. (Proverbs 20:19)

Too Many Words

James reminds us to be slow to speak and Ecclesiastes tells us to not be quick with our mouths.[1] Bottom line, let your words be few. If you cannot bottom line conversations, telling others clearly what and why you say something, then you have a loose tongue. You can be sure, whoever cannot be clear, quick, and to the point in their speech, has much sin to deal with in his or her life.

> When words are many, sin is not absent, but he who holds his tongue is wise. (Proverbs 10:19)

God created light with a few short words, but we ramble on, masking our intentions and excusing ourselves by saying, "That is not what I meant." We can claim that because we are often sinfully unclear in what we said. In your daily conversation learn to mean *yes*, say *yes* and be clear as to what you are "*yesing*." The same goes for *no*. In every conversation, bottom line what you want to say, say what you mean, and then conclude the conversation with a bottom line as to what you meant.

> Above all, my brothers, do not swear—not by heaven or by earth or by anything else. Let your "Yes" be yes, and your "No," no, or you will be condemned. (James 5:12)

Anything more comes from the evil one.

> Simply let your "Yes" be "Yes," and your "No," "No"; anything beyond this comes from the evil one. (Matthew 5:37)

Read the gospels and note how Jesus talked. He always had a point and reached it as quickly as possible. He had no shady areas in His speech. Nor did He weave a loophole so that He could weasel His way out later. How unlike Christ we act. We love to declare long winded stories because we like to hear ourselves talk, get our way, or cover up a hidden sin. Now, I am not talking about rudeness, but clarity and truth. Clarity because love demands that we be honest, clear, and true to what we say at all times.

Here's a great way to practice listening to your own conversation. Before going to church each Sunday, pray that you will "guard your steps when you go to the house of God," to "let your words be few," measuring everything you say before you say it. The church where I pastor doesn't meet for worship until 1:30 in the afternoon, allowing each family and person to wake up refreshed, spend time in prayer, and prepare themselves before attending worship. We sober ourselves up so that we do not offer the "sacrifice of fools" who remain unaware that all the praise, singing, and worship is wrong because we talk too easily and too much.

> Guard your steps when you go to the house of God. Go near to listen rather than to offer the sacrifice of fools, who do not know that they do wrong. Do not be quick with your mouth, do not be hasty in your heart to utter anything before God. God is in heaven and you are on earth, so let your words be few. (Ecclesiastes 5:1–2)

If you are not few with your words then you already have much to examine and surrender to the Lord. Remember, take an intent look into the law of Christ. The following questions only provide a shallow starting point.

Have you ever:

- Changed a story to make yourself look better, whether by mistake or on purpose?[2]
- Felt irritated with someone and not confessed your irritation to them?[3]
- Talked about those God disciplines?[4]
- Had a bad attitude about someone and didn't confess it to them?[5]
- Been correct on an issue and didn't have permission from the Holy Spirit to speak about it, but talked anyway?[6]
- Hated a message brought to you and didn't like the way it was done?[7]
- Thought a person couldn't be that "good," or that a ministry sounded too good to be true?
- Tried to hunt down and prove that someone was sinful?[8]
- Loved someone, but became poisoned by others to hate them?[9]
- Felt positively correct about a conversation, but refused to see something in your flesh that caused you to hear it wrong?[10]
- Didn't understand something happening within the church and blamed the leadership?[11]
- Traveled from person to person, or place to place to make certain everyone understood your point of view?[12]
- Flat-out lied about someone?[13]
- Cursed someone or hoped for evil to take hold of them?[14]
- Caused division in a church because your sin was exposed?[15]
- Had casual conversations, attitudes, or rebellion that led to starting a bitter root in a church?

- Felt upset with someone and thought of them as a "fool"?[16]
- Left a group or church because you were in your flesh?[17]

Taming the Tongue

If you were honest with yourself and God in answering these questions, then you should realize you have an untamed tongue. For all your effort, zeal, and attempts to say the correct thing, your talk is still out of control. Why? Because it is impossible for a man to tame his own tongue. On the other hand, perhaps you pride yourself on being a quiet, reserved individual who doesn't say much. Your tongue still remains untamed in the Lord because you refuse to love others enough to open up your life and be crucified for them. Jesus has no room for self-righteous smugness. God can bless us with control to tame our tongues, but we must admit the truth about our need to change.

> All kinds of animals, birds, reptiles and creatures of the sea are being tamed and have been tamed by man, but no man can tame the tongue. It is a restless evil, full of deadly poison. With the tongue we praise our Lord and Father, and with it we curse men, who have been made in God's likeness. Out of the same mouth come praise and cursing. My brothers, this should not be. (James 3:7–10)

Without a full surrender to God, in all areas of our lives, we will never tame our tongues. How and why we use words reflects our status, or depth of death to self in Christ. The man or woman that can keep a tight reign on his or her tongue controls their whole body. If you want to know how perfect you stand in the Lord, examine your conversation with the Light the Holy Spirit gives. A perfect man can control his tongue. Those who cast slurs or spread evil suspicions are not well off in the Lord, to say the least.

> We all stumble in many ways. If anyone is never at fault in what he says, he is a perfect man, able to keep his whole body in check. (James 3:2)

Once this surrender starts it is not hard to identify the gossips and bitter root individuals. For on the one hand they praise God, but on the other hand they curse men. They enjoy, even if with false humility, the tearing down of another's character. Many who leave churches claiming they were burnt are famous for this. Scripture tells us to test everything, and whenever you listen to a conversation, ask yourself by the power of the Holy Spirit, "Is there some sin this person seeks to avoid in their life? Why is she or he cursing another?" Then listen carefully for the reply of the Holy Spirit for it will save yourself and maybe the one speaking.

Steps of Repentance

How should we repent of gossip, or being taken in by those who have infected us with a bitter root? Here are a few scriptural suggestions:

1. Come fully into the Light, before God and man with all you have done.[18]
2. Do not hold onto any thought that you are right on some point.[19]

3. Realize, if your correctness led to sin because of your attitude, then you are 100% guilty.[20]
4. As the Lord leads, you must speak to those you defiled, confessing your sin. Be careful not to be taken back in again by those who continue to hold onto their sin.[21]
5. You must never, ever speak to the person who started the bitter root until they fully repent. Allow someone else stronger in the Lord to bring this person to repentance. Remember, you were taken in by them once.[22]
6. You must never associate with or talk to those who continue in the slander, slurs, or bitter roots.[23] Do not fool yourself into thinking you are strong enough to resist, because God's Word has declared there is no other way to survive. Or do you think you can be righteous by rebelling against God's Word?
7. Do not even eat lunch with those who will not fully repent of the sin of gossip.[24]
8. Prepare yourself to join with true followers of God and suffer the same kind of slander you helped to spread.
9. Repay the truth four times the amount you lied. Never tire of telling others how wrong you were and the real truth. Go out of your way to make things right. Just as slander is a public sin, so is the repentance process. Everyone must know you sinned and repented. You must "stand up" so that everyone knows your guilt and that God forgives you. Remember, aim to repay four times the good as the harm you did.[25]
10. Ask God to show you daily how you believe and spread half-truths. Plead with God that your "Yes" will be "Yes" and your "No" be "No." Anything other than this comes from the "evil one."[26]

11. Pray hard for the Holy Spirit to control your tongue and reveal how you slur individuals in "small" ways. Ask God to show you how often you curse individuals by calling them "stupid," "ugly," "weird," or whatever personality traits you don't like.[27]
12. Finally, and most importantly, ask God to show you what about your flesh caused you to be taken in by these sins. Plead with God to crucify and put to death all areas of your flesh vulnerable to the sin of gossip. Ask God to send you His Light so you can see what makes you stumble. Otherwise, Satan will come back to take you captive again. Do not rationalize your sin of gossip for even angels do not slander Satan.

> But even the archangel Michael, when he was disputing with the devil about the body of Moses, did not dare to bring a slanderous accusation against him, but said, "The Lord rebuke you!" (Jude 9)

Broken Relationship with God

It is critical for you to understand that if you listen to a false witness, your relationship with God stands on hold until you repent. Indeed, your salvation and relationship with God stopped the day you became a part of those sins. Remember, God will forever destroy anyone who repeats or merely listens to a false witness. Let me quote it again:

> A false witness will perish, and whoever listens to him will be destroyed forever. (Proverbs 21:28)

God has not answered your prayers and guided your life. You have been on your own, doing your own religious or pagan thing. It doesn't matter how much you speak in tongues, or what doors you think God opened for you, for in reality God opposes you until you make this sin right. If you do not see this as true, you remain trapped in your sin and do not understand anything about the truth. Just read how God says you will be put in prison for being angry and slurring your brother—let alone being taken in by a false witness.

> You have heard that it was said to the people long ago, "Do not murder, and anyone who murders will be subject to judgment." But I tell you that anyone who is angry with his brother will be subject to judgment. Again, anyone who says to his brother, "Raca," is answerable to the Sanhedrin. But anyone who says, "You fool!" will be in danger of the fire of hell. Therefore, if you are offering your gift at the altar and there remember that your brother has something against you, leave your gift there in front of the altar. First go and be reconciled to your brother; then come and offer your gift. Settle matters quickly with your adversary who is taking you to court. Do it while you are still with him on the way, or he may hand you over to the judge, and the judge may hand you over to the officer, and you may be thrown into prison. I tell you the truth, you will not get out until you have paid the last penny. (Matthew 5:21–26)

Indeed, you will never escape if you don't repent. Stop what you are doing, leave your gift at church and reconcile with your brother. God will not release those who fail to heed the words of Jesus, Christian or non-Christian, until they have paid the "last penny."

If you listen to some information that a person presents, then fully prepare yourself to take the following steps to completion. Christians must do everything with all their hearts, so those talking to you should know that you will, with great zeal, make sure this comes to a righteous conclusion. If you do not willingly do this, then stop the conversation and tell them you don't want to hear anything more. If you feel that God has made something your business, then the following few guidelines should occur.

1. Let the gossiper know you serve justice alone and if he is deficient in some area of righteousness you will demand he repent.[28]
2. Ask for all the information a person has and listen carefully. It is important you hear all the information at once so that the story cannot be changed later.[29]
3. Ask the Holy Spirit which scriptures apply to the person talking to you.[30]
4. Tell the gossiper you will get back with him to make sure he has gone to the individual he talked about.[31]
5. Follow up to be sure everything happened in a holy way.[32]
6. Let both parties know your final judgment as soon as possible. It is neither loving nor of God to let the matter just hang in silence. Remember, the Law and the Prophets are summed up in doing to others as you would have done to yourself.[33]

As a pastor I hear lots of different stories and my goal in any situation is to resolve the matter as quickly as possible before the Lord. Whatever the turmoil, the gossip must fall to the ground and die. In short, we either bury the story so that the person can forget what is behind and press on toward the goal,[34] or the gossiper must go back to the person that sinned against them and finish the confrontation. All of this is done in the most private and loving manner as the Holy Spirit directs.

CHAPTER 10

What to Talk About

Everyone wants to know what a church believes, but we should first listen to what they talk about, for that tells us what they live. Think of discernment ministries, or even your own church. What would people hear if they came to your church and just listened. In fact, sometime, try doing it yourself and make a note of what people discuss. For we have plenty to talk about in the Lord, but seldom is that heard in the church.

When was the last time you heard members in your church talk to one another with psalms, hymns, and spiritual songs? Have you ever witnessed groups of people huddled around talking about a spiritual song? Now, I don't mean the vile stuff passed off today as Christian music, but spiritual songs that convict the heart and enliven the spirit—music that keeps the soul joyfully on the cross. Songs like

Lift High the Cross that contain words with real meaning, born of knowing the sufferings of the cross:

> Lift high the cross; the love of Christ proclaim,
> Till all the world adore His sacred name.
> Come, Christians, follow where our Savior trod.[1]

Ephesians tells us we should, with joy, use such things in our conversations with each other. God has provided them for us, so let our conversation be a quiet form of singing.

> Speak to one another with psalms, hymns and spiritual songs. Sing and make music in your heart to the Lord, always giving thanks to God the Father for everything, in the name of our Lord Jesus Christ. (Ephesians 5:19–20)

All of this talk occurs while we make music in our hearts to the Lord. When a church has this kind of conversation and music, it is virtually impossible for even the seeds of a bitter root to remain on the ground. Praise and thanksgiving to God eats up such seeds and no matter how tough the message of the cross, you will not hear a word of grumbling. Since music fills the hearts, conversations can't help but be holy. Instead of talking about the latest fashion, TV, movies, other groups, or individuals, the conversation remains wholesome and builds others up in Christ. Admonishments and rebukes are thus surrounded by words of praise, joy, and thanksgiving. Remember well that only the Holy Spirit, by way of the crucified life, can work this in your life or church. Don't attempt to mock; that would only result in sudden spiritual death.

Grieving the Spirit

Ask a simple question about your own conversations: Do they benefit those who listen to walk deeper in Christ or merely give you opportunity to vent bitterness? If you answer with the latter, then it is simply unwholesome talk. Become very sensitive to the emotions of the Holy Spirit so that you can sense when you have grieved Him. Many times I feel a twinge of pain when I have said something or am about to declare something. This is the Holy Spirit warning me not to grieve Him.

> Do not let any unwholesome talk come out of your mouths, but only what is helpful for building others up according to their needs, that it may benefit those who listen. And do not grieve the Holy Spirit of God, with whom you were sealed for the day of redemption. (Ephesians 4:29–30)

A church filled with the love of the Holy Spirit, by way of the cross, will have plenty of bruises and welts. Learning to be dead enough to self to love each other as Christ loves requires much suffering. This bruising can easily cause us to become embittered because many times we must forgive or overlook a brother or sister's sin. It may take years before God comes back to deal with the person's weakness and sin. In fact, God may never address the issue that wounded you, but quietly transform the individual. If you want your pound of justice you will not love the one who offended you, and thus hinder the grace of God. Therefore, remove all bitterness, rage, and anger, forgiving each other just as God forgave you.

> Get rid of all bitterness, rage and anger, brawling and slander, along with every form of malice. Be kind and compassionate to one another, forgiving each other, just as in Christ God forgave you. (Ephesians 4:31–32)

This is crucial to the health of any group of believers. I know many so embittered and unwilling to give up their pride that they cannot find freedom. Whether the sin committed against them was real or not, it does not matter. God calls us to forgive with sweeping, wide strokes of love and mercy. Naturally, we are not talking about whitewash but pure, holy love that encourages and promotes holiness.

Scripture calls us to be imitators of God and live a life of love. It commands us to give ourselves up—our pride, our justifications, our comforts, our demands for justice—and to become a fragrant offering of sacrifice to God. This is what others in the church and the world should see within and outside the walls of the church.

> Be imitators of God, therefore, as dearly loved children and live a life of love, just as Christ loved us and gave himself up for us as a fragrant offering and sacrifice to God. (Ephesians 5:1–2)

Pay No Attention

As a pastor I have heard, directly and indirectly, many things about myself. Comments about my sermons and even how I dress and smile have all been discussed. Many a negative comment has been made; mostly without the person really giving any thought to what he or she said. Even by those I love the most, those I know that love me in the Lord, comments have been made that cut to the quick. Many, many times the Holy Spirit speaks to me of Ecclesiastes 7, reminding me at how quickly I too have voiced an opinion and mouthed off a comment.

> Do not pay attention to every word people say, or you may hear your servant cursing you—for you know in your heart that many times you yourself have cursed others. (Ecclesiastes 7:21–22)

What peace the Lord grants me because He has taught me to "not pay attention" to every word. While many mean the evil things they speak, many more speak without thinking. In our sinful condition we say so much that should not be said. This wisdom gives me patience, and so in Jesus, it becomes glorious to "overlook an offense." How more easily this can happen in a church where individuals make music in their hearts and speak songs and hymns to each other.

> A man's wisdom gives him patience; it is to his glory to overlook an offense. (Proverbs 19:11)

Peace of Christ

Bearing with each other does not mean we grit our teeth and grudgingly endure each other's company. It means in Jesus I can, by God's mercy, truly love others who I would have hated in the world. Think of God's forgiveness. Do you want God to forgive, but only begrudgingly? No, we want God to throw open His arms and love us. We can put on this virtue of love in Christ. As the verse below declares we must "let the peace of Christ rule." The peace of Christ attempts to rule in our hearts and conversations but we will just not let it. We either want to hold onto a grudge or our flesh desires something, causing fights and quarrels.[2] Keeping our minds on worldly things only produces unholy friction.

> Bear with each other and forgive whatever grievances you may have against one another. Forgive as the Lord forgave you. And over all these virtues put on love, which binds them all together in perfect unity. Let the peace of Christ rule in your hearts, since as members of one body you were called to peace. And be thankful. Let the word of Christ dwell in you richly as you teach and admonish one another with all wisdom, and as you sing psalms, hymns and spiritual songs with gratitude in your hearts to God. And whatever you do, whether in word or deed, do it all in the name of the Lord Jesus, giving thanks to God the Father through him. (Colossians 3:13–17)

Once we put on all of this peace and love then we can let the "word of Christ dwell" in us "richly." But how many, like the Pharisees of old, know the Scriptures but sorely miss the virtue of a cross carrying, selfless love? Little wonder such churches are legalistic, dry, and joyless. God calls a Christian to peace, and out of that peace will flow an attitude of thankfulness. As a result, the Holy Spirit applies Scripture as He sees fit.

This thankfulness wells up in everyone as they teach and admonish each other with the wisdom God provides by the Holy Spirit.

All of this teaching, speaking, and admonishing intermingles with the singing of psalms, hymns, and spiritual songs. And if praise and joy were not enough, extreme gratitude explodes from the heart towards God. As stated before, I have known a church that destroyed itself with bitter roots. God, in His mercy, brought me to a church where this gratitude fills so much, that it is almost impossible for a bitter root, gossip, or slur to occur. If one does start, the Holy Spirit rebukes it and we pour praise upon the thankfulness we have for God that He would bless us by keeping us clean and holy.

Finally, what is there to talk about if we don't gossip? The answer is simple and unending—the goodness of God! Get busy talking of the goodness of God and much will fall into its proper place. Let us speak all day long of God's righteousness and goodness and there will never be room for gossip.

> My tongue will speak of your righteousness and of your praises all day long. (Psalm 35:28)

Let us do so "all day long."

CHAPTER II

When You Are Slandered

Gossip, slander, bitter roots, and betrayal—some or all—may fall upon those faithful to Jesus Christ. However, as we have seen clearly none will be exempt from feeling the sting of at least one. Satan eagerly waits to slander any good deed performed out of love for Jesus. How then shall we respond?

I cannot lay down a lot of rules. Each situation is unique and the battle belongs to the Lord. Most of the time, it reaches beyond our power to stop the gossip or to answer back, making gossip a cowardly act. Those who use this wicked tool know this and relish the use of darkness to further their agenda. Most importantly, put your faith in God. It is tempting to fret about what others will say or do next, which only leads to evil.

> Refrain from anger and turn from wrath; do not fret—it leads only to evil. (Psalms 37:8)

The pattern tends to go like this. We hear of some gossip and keep turning it over and over in our heads. *What did they say? Who have they told? What will they say next?* All of this nervous anxiety leads to anger. Then the evil one can easily stir us up to wrath. Satan knows that if he can lead a disciple of Jesus to grow angry, then the love of Jesus is quenched.

Trusting the Lord to work the victory means that your victory will be complete. This allows God to work mercy upon those who might repent of such sins and, at the same time, your love becomes heaping coals to those who harden themselves against the love of Christ shown through you. Consider—what is the worst that can happen? Death? A loss of reputation? An opportunity to talk about Jesus with others who come to you about the gossip and in the end God Himself defends you?

Wait on God

Let us read the passage that surrounds the one we just looked at. As you read over the scripture before the Lord, focus in on the words, "wait patiently." Just waiting is not enough, we must become so dead to our sinful nature that we wait with a quiet, calm, and patient spirit for the Lord to do something. We can do this not only because Jesus stills the storms that rage in our souls, but in a "little while" you will look for the wicked and will not find them. Though they "plot" with gnashing teeth they will soon gnash their teeth in hell for the slander they slung at God's children.

> Be still before the Lord and wait patiently for him; do not fret when men succeed in their ways, when they carry out their wicked schemes. Refrain from anger and turn from wrath; do not fret—it leads only to evil. For evil men will be cut off, but those who hope in the Lord will inherit the land. A little while, and the wicked will be no more; though you look for them, they will not be found. But the meek will inherit the land and enjoy great peace. The wicked plot against the righteous and gnash their teeth at them; (Psalm 37:7–12)

Let us take note that often those who gossip, slander, betray, or are entangled by a bitter root "succeed" in their evil plans. It takes some real faith in God to wait for Him when such men can carry out and prosper in their plans. Only the meek and those who peacefully wait upon God will inherit the land. The delusion of the wicked's victory is but a moment and they will certainly lose the war. More than that, the victory they rejoice in will become an eternal defeat that they will regret forever. They will forever feel ashamed that they even won a single battle.

How can we make ourselves rest at peace? We can't, but the Holy Spirit more than willingly can. God may allow you to wrestle with your fretting and your desire to defend yourself, but deny yourself and put your faith in God. In His timing the Holy Spirit will take control of your mind and work the peace of Christ. After all, Jesus is the Prince of Peace. Surrender the control of your mind and let God control it by the Holy Spirit.

> The mind of sinful man is death, but the mind controlled by the Spirit is life and peace; (Romans 8:6)

The Lord is always very near, and even more so when we suffer the scorn of evil men for the sake of righteousness. Since we know this to be true we can remain gentle and not feel anxious about anything. As we deny ourselves the luxury of feeling anxious, we can talk to God who will guard not only our hearts, but our minds as well. His divine power will keep us in perfect peace.

If you come to God without grumbling and overflowing with thanksgiving no matter what the situation, the peace of God will "guard" your heart and mind. In fact, you will say to yourself in wonderment, "I should be worried, but I am not." You will find yourself in a very strange situation and sense that God guards your very spirit and soul.

> Let your gentleness be evident to all. The Lord is near. Do not be anxious about anything, but in everything, by prayer and petition, with thanksgiving, present your requests to God. And the peace of God, which transcends all understanding, will guard your hearts and your minds in Christ Jesus. (Philippians 4:5–7)

Join in the Suffering

There is no use in looking for help from any man. As discussed, rarely will anyone take a stand against gossip and dig up a bitter root. Most simply remain too selfish, in the name of Jesus, to suffer on the behalf of those slandered. Rarely will a church or ministry strike against gossip when it is not self-serving to do so. They do not serve justice for the sake of justice or the interest of a wounded party.[1] The selfless love of Christ, that willingly risks reputation or job over some struggle of gossip inflicted upon another, is so rare that it is almost nonexistent. In short, the church will not act to stop the gossip unless it benefits in some way. In fact, most are fearful that the gossip will rub off on them, and they value the approval of men more than the approval of God. They should rejoice with those slandered but instead they avoid them, which is the first goal of the gossiper. The love of Jesus should move us to lay down our lives for our slandered brothers and sisters. God, however, will not force us to do it. He will not tell someone they must stand by, defend, or publicly support those maligned. He gives us a free choice to love or not to love. Therefore Paul gave Timothy the opportunity to join in the sufferings of Christ. Does the love of Christ move you to suffer with those who suffer the sting of gossip because of the gospel? If not, why not?

> So do not be ashamed to testify about our Lord, or ashamed of me his prisoner. But join with me in suffering for the gospel, by the power of God. (2 Timothy 1:8)

Few indeed have enough spiritual insight to call attention to people who gossip without being taken in by their words. If you seek the help of others, it could drag them down into the mud, haggling about words, fine hairpin points, and issues that concern everything but the heart of the situation. You might convince someone to take your side concerning the particulars of the gossip, only for them to be swayed later when talking to the gossiper. This happens because the church has lost its power to deal with the heart as the Holy Spirit gives illumination. We judge everything by mere appearance and outward debates, and accomplish nothing in the Lord.[2] This unspiritual condition in the church caused Paul a great deal of concern.[3]

Do Not Defend Yourself

Deny yourself and do not attempt to clear yourself by revealing personal information about someone else. Though they may have gossiped about personal things in your life, do not sin by declaring personal things about theirs. If you do, you only close the door of repentance a little bit more and harden those that might repent later. To others you only demonstrate you are just as sinful as those who attack you. Such a bad reputation cannot easily be undone.

> If you argue your case with a neighbor, do not betray another man's confidence, or he who hears it may shame you and you will never lose your bad reputation. (Proverbs 25:9–10)

Let me be more clear; this is not to say that you never reveal private things you know, for to everything there is a time and season.[4] But the self that would defend itself must be crucified to know when to speak up for your rights. Like Paul, who appealed to Caesar, but only because he needed to die in Rome. Or when Paul was in Thyatira he demanded that the city leaders escort them out for violating their rights, but only after he had been severely beaten and preached to the jailer. If you feel uncertain that self is on the cross or if the Holy Spirit speaks through you, then remain silent and suffer the injustice. If you take the plank out of your own eye, speak boldly and clearly as the Holy Spirit guides. But never, ever fall for the temptation Satan will lay before you to come down off the cross and defend yourself. Remember, if you are filled with the righteousness of Christ, then it is not you they slander, but God. And He will repay.

> A false witness will not go unpunished, and he who pours out lies will perish. (Proverbs 19:9)

If the gossip is true, then repent with godly sorrow,[5] thanking God that He sent an enemy to carry away your dross. Confess your sin to God, man, and to the person gossiping, before you deal with their sins. Remember to take the plank out of your own eye first.

Even if you are innocent about the gossip, others could say plenty about you if they saw your heart. Let us humble ourselves like David; though he was innocent of the stones thrown at him and could easily have struck a death blow back, he let injustice continue so that God could work His justice in the situation. Do not fear, God will see injustice, and if you are innocent, He will repay.

> David then said to Abishai and all his officials, "My son, who is of my own flesh, is trying to take my life. How much more, then, this Benjamite! Leave him alone; let him curse, for the Lord has told him to. It may be that the Lord will see my distress and repay me with good for the cursing I am receiving today." So

> David and his men continued along the road while Shimei was going along the hillside opposite him, cursing as he went and throwing stones at him and showering him with dirt. (2 Samuel 16:11–13)

Delight in God's Word

Let me end this chapter with this word of counsel. When slandered, ignore the gossip and meditate upon the commands of God. Through all the many times I have been slandered, I ran back to God. If the charge was false or too cruel to take heed of, it still caused me to recount my ways and discover fresh in the Lord how I needed to repent and cleanse my heart. I found peace, joy, and freedom in meditating and taking great delight in the statues of God.

> Though rulers sit together and slander me, your servant will meditate on your decrees. Your statutes are my delight; they are my counselors. I am laid low in the dust; preserve my life according to your word. I recounted my ways and you answered me; teach me your decrees. (Psalm 119:23–26)

Though rulers sit together and slander you, think not on their evil talk, but upon the goodness of God's decrees. Let God's statues bring you delight instead of feeling depressed because others speak evil of your name. Joyful obedience to God will increase in your life and you will praise God for allowing even kings to slander you—for they drove you into His loving arms.

Everything Said

May the conversation in the church give the Lord deep pleasure.

> Then those who feared the Lord talked with each other, and the Lord listened and heard. A scroll of remembrance was written in his presence concerning those who feared the Lord and honored his name. (Malachi 3:16)

Endnotes

Introduction

1. 1 Corinthians 5:11
2. Luke 12:51
3. Matthew 12:30

Chapter 1: World of Evil

1. *Roadside Photographs, Here at the Table,* by Joshua Williams, UPC 5661349282
2. Colossians 4:6
3. We're not talking about obvious public sins which the Holy Spirit might lead someone to renounce openly. Whether the sin is/was public or private, it is never left up to us if we speak ill of another. We can never play God. We must die to self so that if we speak it is not us, but Jesus who speaks. Therefore scripture says we should speak only using the very words of Christ (see 1 Peter 4:11).
4. John 12:25
5. 1 John 1:7
6. Hosea 12:6
7. Acts 15:1 Corinthians 2:2, 1 Timothy 6:5

8. 1 Timothy 5:21
9. Proverbs 11:13
10. Luke 12:2

Chapter 2: An Art Form

1. Romans 3:13
2. John 13:34–35
3. Psalm 109:5
4. Galatians 5:11
5. 1 Corinthians 13:7
6. Matthew 24:12
7. John 6:66
8. *eau de Cult*, by Timothy Williams, ISBN 1-57921-511-4
9. Psalm 37:6

Chapter 3: Slurs

1. Proverbs 18:2
2. 1 John 5:16
3. John 7:6
4. John 7:24
5. John 6:63
6. *Hating for Jesus*, by Timothy Williams,
   Soft cover: ISBN 1-57921-756-7
   Hard cover: ISBN 1-57921-646-3
7. *eau de Cult*, by Timothy Williams, ISBN 1-57921-511-4
8. Acts 24:5

Chapter 4: Poisoned Minds

1. Psalm 15:2
2. Acts 3:26
3. 1 Corinthians 1:17
4. Psalm 55:21, Proverbs 27:6

5. *Bad Fruit*, by Timothy Williams, Soft cover: ISBN 1-57921-556-4 Hard cover: ISBN 1-57921-638-2
6. Romans 1:5
7. Romans 1:5

Chapter 5: A False Witness

1. Romans 3:13
2. 1 Corinthians 5:11
3. 2 Timothy 1:8
4. Job 42:5–6
5. Philippians 2:3
6. 1 Thessalonians 5:21
7. Jude 16
8. Acts 3:26
9. John 2:25
10. 1 Peter 4:1

Chapter 6: Bitter Roots

1. John 6:60
2. Acts 14:22
3. Matthew 7:1
4. Example of Grumbling and Complaining.
   Exodus 5:13 Moses wanted God to send someone else.
   Exodus 5:20 Israel complained about making bricks with no straw.
   Exodus 6:9 They would not listen to Moses because of their discouragement.
   Exodus 14:11 "Because there were no graves in Egypt you brought us here to die."
   Exodus 15:24 Israel grumbled about no water.
   Exodus 16:2 They wanted meat.
   Exodus 16:7–8 Moses said God heard their grumbling.
   Exodus 17:2–3 They were thirsty.
   Exodus 32:7 They grumbled because Moses took too long on the mountain.

Numbers 11:1–3 They complained about their hardships.

Numbers 11:4–6 They craved other food.

Numbers 11:10–15 Moses complained that the people were too great of a burden.

Numbers 12:1–2 Miriam and Aaron complained about Moses' Cushite wife.

Numbers 13:28–29 After the report of the Promised Land, they said, "The people who live there are too powerful."

Numbers 13:31–33 They complained "The people are too big."

Numbers 14:1–4 Weeping and grumbling about entering the land. "If only we had died in Egypt!"

Numbers 14:10 They wanted to stone Moses.

Numbers 14:27–29 God heard their grumbling.

Numbers 14:36–37 God killed the men who spread a bad report.

Numbers 16:1–3 Korah's rebellion. They wanted to be the religious leaders.

Numbers 16:12–15 They accused Moses of lording his authority over them.

Numbers 16:41 The people accused Moses of killing Korah.

Numbers 20:2–5 They wanted water.

Numbers 21:4–5 They wanted bread and water, they were tired of manna.

Numbers 32:5 The Rubenites and Gadites did not want to cross the Jordan.

Deuteronomy 1:26–28 "The Lord brought us out of Egypt to deliver us to the Amorites."

Deuteronomy 28:47 They did not serve joyfully and gladly.

Joshua 7:7–9 Joshua complained because they lost the battle at Ai.

Joshua 17:14 People of Joseph complained about their allotment.

Judges 8:1 The Ephraimites complained against Gideon.

1 Samuel 8:4, 19 They wanted a king.

1 Samuel 9:18 They grumbled because the leaders would not attack the Gibeonites.

1 Samuel 10:27 Troublemakers complained about Saul.

1 Samuel 17:28 David's brothers grumbled against him.
1 Samuel 18:8–9 Saul complained because David got more credit that he did.
1 Samuel 22:7–8 Saul grumbled about David.
1 Samuel 22:13 Saul complained about Ahimelech.
1 Samuel 25:10–11 Nabal complained about sharing with David.
2 Samuel 15:2–4 Absalom complained about David.
Psalm 78 A recap of the Israelites history of grumbling.
Psalm 106 Another recap of several instances of grumbling by the Israelites.
Isaiah 40:27 Israel complained that God disregarded their cause.
Isaiah 58:3 The people complained that God didn't see their fasting.
Isaiah 58:9b The Israelites pointed their fingers and talked maliciously.
Jeremiah 26:7–9 They complained about Jeremiah's prophesies.
Jeremiah 44:16-18 They complained that everything was fine when they sacrificed to the Queen of Heaven.
Jonah 4:1-3 Jonah complained that God showed mercy.
Malachi 1:12–13 The people complained about the Lord's table.

5. 1 Corinthians 5:8
6. Romans 8:28
7. Acts 3:26
8. 2 Corinthians 13:11
9. Of course this passage can be used to keep honest questions from being asked in a church, but we are not talking about that sin.

Chapter 7: Betrayers and Parent Cursers

1. Proverbs 16:6

Chapter 9: Look in the Mirror

1. James 1:19
2. Matthew 12:34
3. Ephesians 4:3

4. Psalm 69:26
5. James 5:16
6. John 8:28
7. Luke 7:32
8. Matthew 15:19, Zechariah 7:10
9. 2 Peter 3:16–17, 1 Thessalonians 3:6–8
10. Proverbs 14:6–8
11. 2 Corinthians 1:14
12. Acts 14:19
13. John 8:44
14. Proverbs 26:2
15. 3 John 1:9–10
16. Matthew 5:22
17. Ephesians 4:3, James 5:9
18. 1 John 1:7
19. Job 42:7
20. Hebrews 12:15
21. Galatians 6:1
22. Galatians 6:1
23. 2 Timothy 3:1–5
24. 1 Corinthians 5:11
25. 2 Timothy 1:8, Luke 19:8
26. Matthew 5:37, James 5:12
27. Matthew 5:22
28. Deuteronomy 16:20
29. Proverbs 18:17
30. John 7:24
31. Luke 17:3
32. 2 Corinthians 13:2
33. Matthew 7:12
34. Philippians 3:13

Chapter 10: What to Talk About

1. *Life High the Cross*, words by George W. Kitchin, modified by Michael R. Newbolt in 1916.

2. James 4:1

Chapter 11: When You Are Slandered

1. Deuteronomy 16:20
2. John 7:24
3. 1 Corinthians 6:5
4. Ecclesiastes 3:1
5. 2 Corinthians 7:10–11

Other Books by Timothy Williams

timothy@newdayministry.org

Even the Demons Believe

- A small book that details how to get started in the new life of Christ.
  ISBN 1-57921-355-3

Insanity in the Church

- The church has gone insane with all of its boasting, love of pleasure, money, and other insanities. Find out why this happens, how to recognize insanity, and most importantly, how to become sane in Christ.
  ISBN 1-57921-390-1

A Whisper Revival

- How to prepare yourself for revival when God moves, as well as what dangers to look for.
  ISBN 1-57921-274-3

101 Ways to Deny Self

- This book is based on 1 Peter 1:13 where we are called to prepare our minds for action. It is not a list of rules, but a preparation for the Holy Spirit to guide us in joyful obedience.
  ISBN 1-57921-397-9

Hating for Jesus (John 12:25)

- A very hard hitting, detailed book about the offensive message of the cross. It is a difficult read and one will have to persevere to get through it. If the reader does, rich joy will be found.
  Soft cover: ISBN 1-57921-756-7
  Hard cover: ISBN 1-57921-646-3

eau de Cult – The Fragrance of Love in the First Church

- This book explains the fruit of God's love being worked in a body of believers, and how many will consider that to look like a cult.
  ISBN 1-57921-511-4

Bewitchment – You Foolish Galatians

- While this book is written to a specific denomination it really is a call to all of us to be sure we are walking in the Spirit and not human effort.
  ISBN 1-57921-469-X

Prosperity Teachers

- This book reveals how and when God gives us the desires of our hearts. It will cause you to carefully examine what the Bible teaches on prosperity.
  ISBN 1-57921-489-4

Bad Fruit

- This book examines both sides of the "once saved, always saved" debate and discusses the fruit produced in the lives of those who believe they can never fall from grace.
  Soft cover: ISBN 1-57921-556-4
  Hard cover: ISBN 1-57921-638-2

Bad Fruit Study Guide

- This study guide is a companion to the book *Bad Fruit: The Result of Once Saved Always Saved.* It's written to help you better understand what's written in *Bad Fruit* and will encourage you to apply what you have learned to your own life, experience, and relationship with God.
  ISBN 1-57921-721-4

Ears to Hear

- *Ears to Hear* explores how we can know for sure we've heard God's voice and not another voice. This book will point you to the cross of Christ that causes our hearts to tune into God's voice correctly.
  Soft cover: ISBN 1-57921-718-4
  Hard cover: ISBN 1-57921-720-6

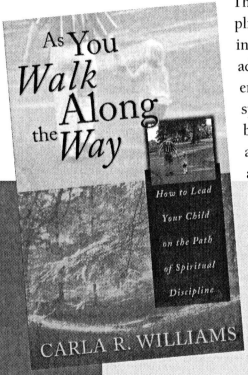

To order additional copies of

GOSSIP *and the* GOSPEL

call

Toll free: (877) 421-READ (7323)

Printed in the United States
42004LVS00003B/2